Praise for

Discover the Power of Laughter

"Stunning, engaging, and *timely*. This book has the possibility to lead the world away from pain and suffering and to transform a life from humdrum to amazing. I am grateful for the emphasis on *choice*. How many people really know laughing is a choice?"

—Lou Hopson,
retired US Army Colonel, Atlanta

"Sarah and Rachael have articulated in the finest fashion not only the importance of laughter but also how to participate in laughter to heal oneself. I was one of Jacqueline's doctors during her stay at Duke University Hospital. At times I wanted to cry, but Sarah and Jacqueline showed me how to pull myself back together and laugh."

—Dr. Terry Harville,
MD, PhD D (ABMLI) F(ACHI),
University of Arkansas for Medical Sciences

"As a COVID survivor with significant lung damage, currently living on supplemental oxygen, I am always looking for ways to improve my lungs. Since reading *Discover the Power of Laughter*, I laugh out loud every day and can sense the difference it makes in my lung capacity. Getting into a good habit was difficult at first, but the tools provided in this book—Smile-Ups and Laughter Breaths—made the process easy."

—Cherryl Galezewski,
CEO, Pass Along Gifts

Identical twins Sarah and Rachael are a unifying force for the power of laughter. Now, they have gone MAD!—Making a Difference—with this book filled with their personal stories and *Laughter Games*.

—Barry Shore, The Ambassador of Joy,
author of *The Joy of Living: How to Slay Stress and Be Happy*,
host of *Joy of Living* podcast

"When I was having the hardest time of my life, my country [Ukriane] was in the midst of a full-scale war. Sarah convinced me to laugh with her for 5 minutes. It sounded ridiculous—the people I know may be dying so how could I laugh? It felt ridiculous *not* to—the tension inside me was so strong, I needed to release it. When we laughed together online, time and space disappeared and my heart expanded. I forgot about the war and was fully present in my body. Reading *Discover the Power of Laughter,* I understood how Sarah reframed and learned from the darkest moment of her life just to shine brighter. This book will be helpful to anyone who is going through hard times or simply wants more joy in life. The goodness is inside you, laugh it out loud. The tools are inside the book, use them."

—Katia Kulyk,
Meditation Magician, Coach, Author; Ukraine

"Sarah and Rachael have written a brilliant and important classic! Filled with scientific evidence of why a laughter practice will benefit our lives and relationships, *Discover the Power of Laughter* will inspire you with its raw authenticity, impactful stories, and delightful techniques. Don't keep this book to yourself. It's the perfect gift to share—the gift of laughter.

—Laurie Ellis-Young,
co-founder, BreathLogic, Inc.,
co-author of *Breath Is Life: Taking In and Letting Go*

"I would definitely recommend *Discover the Power of Laughter* to therapists as a resource. The breathing exercises and playful games have been helpful in working with my clients. The games helped me personally move more easily into laughter and tap into my own creative energy."

—Jai Dei Jackson,
psychotherapist, Atlanta

As I began reading *Discover the Power of Laughter,* I really felt like Sarah and Rachael were talking directly to me. Their honesty and openness made it easy for me to connect my story to theirs. Integrating laughter into my personal life has been healing, especially in working through the grief of losing my mother. I highly recommend this book to anyone—especially those who, like me, may feel apprehensive. Sometimes the things in life we avoid, are the things we need the most."

—Stephanie Goldberg,
sixth grade teacher, Queens

I'd planned to skim *Discover the Power of Laughter,* by Rachael and Sarah, but I got hooked by the stories. They are masterful practitioners of extemporaneous laughter whose goal is to spread the joy. In their book, they share their personal struggles, dive into their most painful memories, and explain their life-changing journeys in learning how to laugh for the sake of laughing. Sarah and Rachael have conducted dozens of interviews, examined the literature, and studied the research on all aspects of laughter. They discovered that it might be the one thing in life you can never have too much of!

—G.P. Gottlieb,
author of the *Whipped and Sipped* Mystery Series

"Laughter is a wonderful way to heal deep wounds as well as minor frustrations. An easy read, *Discover the Power of Laughter* is chockfull of great exercises and insights."

—David M. Matthews,
author of *Every Man Sees You Naked:
An Insider's Guide to How Men Think*

"*Discover the Power of Laughter* was like taking a course on laughter—with fun homework! The upbeat rhythm includes a balanced combination of story, games, history, and science/psychology. This book showed me how many more opportunities there are to laugh than I realized."

—Izzy Gesell,
certified professional speaker,
humorologist, author of *Instructional Moments*

"Reading *Discover the Power of Laughter* has helped me understand laughter's value as a powerful tool. The book provides practical ways to create and sustain a laughter habit. Reading both authors' backstories and seeing how laughter helped them through difficulties has inspired me through my own challenges. I can't wait to use it in my teaching, too."

—Adina Simon,
preschool teacher, Hollywood, Florida

"I'd never heard of Laughter Yoga before reading *Discover the Power of Laughter*. It was life-changing. Profound, even. I know that sounds cliché, or even trite, but I don't use these terms lightly. I was astounded to discover the research on laughter, the many techniques to get you laughing, and the many health benefits that result from building a laughter habit."

—Herta Feely,
editor and author of *Saving Phoebe Murrow*

"Grabbing someone else's attention with the *Ha-Ha-Has* of the Laughter Breaths game to remind them to smile and laugh works every time. It automatically gives me the giggles. Thanks for sharing this valuable tip with the world."

—Bob Wheeler,
CFO, The Comedy Store,
host of *Money You Should Ask* podcast

"*Discover the Power of Laughter* is filled with love and spreads joy. Reading it has made me more aware of laughter than ever before. I love the *Laughter Games* Sarah and Rachael have created. They are easy, fun, and great for all ages. I now hear laughter differently and I laugh deeper and more fully because I know the many health benefits I will receive."

—Mecca Page,
co-founder, New World Women, LLC

As a stage IV cancer survivor, I can attest that health challenges can become less arduous when you infuse laughter, joy, and play. Because the co-authors explore these playful concepts from dichotomous world views, whether you're a curmudgeon, class clown, CEO, facilitator, frontline worker, or parent, you can glean exactly what you need from their unique perspectives. There are lots of self-help books, but few explore the topic of laughter in such an intimate, comprehensive, and useful, yet fun way. Read *Discover the Power of Laughter* alone or with a laughter buddy and have a blast!

—Saranne Rothberg,
CEO, The ComedyCures Foundation,
host of *Beating Cancer Daily* podcast,
stage IV cancer survivor

"The knowledge that you can access laughter and its benefits at any time, even when you least feel like laughing, even in the midst of great pain, is a kind of superpower. What other therapy requires no prescription, is free, and comes in limitless supply? Read this book to unlock this superpower for yourself."

—Joseph Rosenthal, Anesthetist

Blessings & Giggles,
Sarah & Rachael

Discover the Power of Laughter

Jump-start your journey to health and joy

Sarah Routman   Rachael Siegelman

MATTERHORN PRESS
Atlanta, GA

Copyright © 2025 by Sarah Routman and Rachael Siegelman

All rights reserved. No part of this publication may be reproduced, distributed, or transmitted in any form or by any means, without the prior written permission of the publisher, except in the case of brief quotations embodied in book reviews.

If you would like permission to use material from this book for other than review purposes, receive volume discounts, or have Sarah or Rachael speak at an event, please contact the publisher at: www.DiscoverThePowerOfLaughter.com

Book cover and interior design by Bookery.design
Photographs are by Sarah Routman unless otherwise listed
Photograph of Sarah and Jacqueline by Brent Routman
Photograph of World Laughter Day by random laughter enthusiast at the park
Author Photographs of Sarah by Block Portrait Studios
Author Photographs of Rachael by Leora Sowell, Moments of Now Photography

Published by Matterhorn Press, Atlanta

Library of Congress Cataloging-in-Publication Data is on file with the publisher.

ISBN 978-1-960889-28-7   Paperback
ISBN 978-1-960889-18-8   eBook
ISBN 978-1-960889-36-2   Audiobook

Printed in the United States of America

Disclaimer:
This book is intended to provide helpful information and pique your curiosity. The authors have made every effort to make sure their research is current, and the links are live. They assume no liability or responsibility for any errors or omissions in this book. Readers are encouraged to conduct their own research as they travel on a laughter-filled path toward well-being and joy.

First Printing, 2025

Contents

Forewords — vii
Invitation — 1

Introduction Doing What Comes Naturally — 3

1 Sarah's Story—Choosing to Laugh — 11
2 Rachael's Story—Choosing *Not* to Laugh — 23
3 Ready or Not, Laugh! — 39
4 Laughter Is More than Child's Play — 67
5 *Laughter Games* — 85
6 Create Your Own *Laughter Games* — 105
7 Laugh When Life Hurts — 119
8 Use Laughter to Cope and Succeed — 143
9 Establish A Laughter Habit — 161
10 Connect and Celebrate With Laughter — 181
11 Laughter Discoveries: Past, Present, Future — 203

Conclusion Laughter Deepens Connection — 225

Alphabetical List of *Laughter Games* — 230
Laughter Games Quick Reference Guide — 232
Additional Resources — 234
Behind the Scenes & Acknowledgments — 255
About the Authors — 262
Index — 264

*For Jacqueline, Peggy, and Grandpa Barney,
whose laughter lives with us still.*

Forewords

Dr. Michael Miller, a cardiologist who prescribes laughter as part of his regular practice, and Dr. Matan Kataria, the founder of Laughter Yoga, offer their perspectives and experiences. We are grateful for their contributions to healing in the world and to this book.

Michael Miller, MD, Cardiologist, Philadelphia, Pennsylvania, USA

Laughter is one of the most powerful tools we have to improve our health and well-being. As a cardiologist, I have seen the transformative effects of laughter on my patients firsthand. As a medical professional who has been researching the impact of laughter for many years, I can attest that the benefits of laughter on vascular health and immune function are well-documented. That's why I am delighted to prescribe fifteen minutes a day of deep belly laughing to all my heart patients. As much as we all love to laugh, incorporating more laughter into our lives can be challenging, especially during stressful times.

How can we change our mindset and overcome the daily stress-based obstacles thrust upon us from various personal, family, and professional angles? *Discover the Power of Laughter,* written by identical twin sisters and laughter experts, Sarah Routman and Rachael Siegelman, is the answer.

This inspirational book provides a practical and easy-to-master, step-by-step approach to bring out your Inner Child. With their hands-on and well-researched approach, they show you how to maximize positive emotions—through smiling, breathing, laughing, clapping, etc.—in new and imaginative ways. The stories and life experiences highlighted in this book will keep you engaged and excited about trying out and incorporating the numerous *Laughter Games* that have been well-tested and thoughtfully designed . . . in other words, it is just what the doctor ordered!

I hope you enjoy this book as much as I did!

Dr. Madan Kataria, Founder, Laughter Yoga, India

I was the youngest of eight children in a family of simple, hardworking farmers. Despite the challenges of rural life, our home was filled with laughter, a natural, spontaneous joy that came from singing, dancing, and celebrating together. This pure, effortless laughter shaped my understanding of happiness. When I moved to a bustling city to fulfill my mother's wish for me to become a doctor, I encountered forced laughter, punctuated by jokes, yet lacking the warmth and connection I had known in my village. This contrast stayed with me and eventually led to the creation of Laughter Yoga, a practice rooted in joyous laughter without the need for humor. It was a return to the simplicity and innocence I had known as a child, where laughter was a natural expression of being together and celebrating life.

In this book, written by identical twin sisters who have dedicated their lives to spreading the gift of laughter, I see a similar journey. Sarah, one of the authors, is one of my Laughter Yoga Ambassadors. Her dedication to this practice reflects a deep understanding of the power of laughter. Just as I discovered the benefits of laughter and its ability to bring joy, relieve stress, and foster connection, Sarah and Rachael have harnessed these insights to create a guide that will help countless others do the same. Their journey in writing this book mirrors my own path of discovery. They recognized that laughter is about connection, joy, and the simple pleasures of life. In a world that often feels rushed, stressed, and disconnected, their book offers a way back to the joy that lies within us all. It is a guide to putting laughter back into our lives, not as an afterthought, but as a central part of our well-being.

I am honored to write this foreword and to support the authors in their mission to spread laughter far and wide. Their work is a continuation of a journey that began in a small village many years ago. I have no doubt that it will touch the lives of many, bringing the healing power of laughter to those who need it most.

Invitation

We invite you to laugh.
Out loud!
Right now!
Just because.

Go ahead...

Take a deep breath, and

Say *Ha-Ha-Ha!*

Laugh, you say? But you didn't tell me a joke. I don't see any cute pictures of babies or puppies playing. And you want me to just laugh, out loud? On purpose?

What if I don't feel like laughing?

How do I just laugh?

Good questions.

Try this: Lift the sides of your mouth into a gentle smile. Imagine a pile of puppies tickling a giggling toddler. If that doesn't trigger a feeling of joy for you, don't worry. It's not about the image.

Allow yourself to smile. Smiling on the outside sets off a chain reaction on the inside, triggering a flood of positive hormones—with virtually no additional effort. Laughing takes it up a notch. Keep smiling, start reading. You're about to discover the power of purposeful, playful laughter.

Introduction

Doing What Comes Naturally

You were born knowing how to laugh. There is some evidence that babies laugh in utero. Even deaf and blind babies laugh. Laughter is the universal language—it needs no translation. Shared laughter connects people despite their differences.

You're about to discover how the simple act of laughing out loud can help ease you through even the most difficult of challenges, improve your health, add joy, and enhance your life. This is not a book of jokes or humor even though our goal is to have you laughing like you've never laughed before.

We're talking about a very specific type of laughter—sustained, purposeful, playful laughter. You may be wondering, *how is that different from what I get when I go to a comedy club?* Humor-based laughter requires external stimulation, a comedian, a joke, or a funny story. Self-generated, purposeful, playful laughter is unique and can be learned. It's the most effective and efficient self-care tool we know, and it has the power to transform your life. It has changed ours in ways we never imagined.

Let us introduce ourselves: We, the co-authors of this book, are identical twins.

Sarah, an artist and educator, is spontaneous, outgoing, and lighthearted. Sarah chose early in life to laugh often.

Rachael is thoughtful, reserved, and serious. No surprise, she's a lawyer. As you'll discover, Rachael chose at a young age not to laugh. Why? Because she was determined to do the opposite of everything Sarah, her younger sister by two minutes, did. Over the years, as she observed Sarah overcome tremendous challenges with positivity and laughter, Rachael realized laughter could help her become more easygoing and positive, more approachable, and ultimately more joyful. She decided to consciously add laughter to her daily routine.

Why laugh? Why regularly? Why intentionally? Laughter is a valuable, life-altering experience. A good round of hearty laughter is not only fun, it also impacts your body and mind in positive ways. Laughter causes chemical changes in your body. Vigorous laughter lowers fight-or-flight hormones, raises feel-good endorphins, increases blood flow, and also stimulates muscles and organs. Laughter pulls you directly into the present, focuses your attention, releases negative emotions, and fills you with joy. Laughing intentionally on a regular basis yields the best results. We've done it ourselves, and we've done the research.

It doesn't matter what prompts your *guffaw* or *ha-ha-ha*. Intentional laughter is self-generated and allows *you* to determine the duration and depth of your laugh, so you can enjoy the greatest rewards, unlike comedy-induced laughter, which lasts only as long as you find the joke to be funny. Both kinds of laughter can be contagious.

In this book, we'll be teaching you about laughter—the power of anticipating laughter, overcoming resistance to laughter, easing into laughter with smiling and breathing, being vulnerable, willing to play, and engaging in full-bodied intentional laughter. We'll review many of the benefits of laughter we uncovered in our research—because we found them informative and compelling.

In **Chapters 1 and 2**, read our stories to understand how twin sisters came to laughter from opposite starting points. You'll discover how we both came to embrace laughter as an empowering tool for life, and you'll find yourself somewhere on the continuum—as someone who laughs easily, like Sarah, or resists laughing at first, like Rachael.

In **Chapter 3,** you'll find our special formula for purposeful, playful laughter, along with warm-up games. We also share some of the personal stories we collected over the past twenty years from people who credit learning to laugh on purpose with their healing, personal growth, or increased happiness—real-life examples of the power and magic of laughter in action.

To persuade you that laughter is a worthwhile practice to engage in regularly, we've given you highlights of our research and discoveries in **Chapter 4.** We hope you'll find the health benefits as compelling as we do.

In **Chapter 5,** we explain some of our favorite *Laughter Games*, and you'll start to notice how laughter can be used in almost any situation in life. Play the games. You'll be glad you did.

To get your imagination flowing, **Chapter 6** is all about how to create *Laughter Games* designed around your own life. Here we share our secret sauce about the steps we take when creating new *Laughter Games,* often in a moment, responding to the stresses and challenges at hand. We take you behind the scenes and walk you through our process so you can see just how we do it. Use our ideas as stepping stones to make up new games of your own. We're confident you'll view life differently after you notice all the playful prompts around you.

Chapters 7 and 8 illustrate how valuable laughter can be to transform negativity into positivity. Laughter is a powerful coping strategy. We designed the games in these chapters to respond to situations in our own lives. These games not only show you the power of laughter to reduce stress and reframe your life, they show you more examples of how we invent new games. You'll get an inside view of games that help reduce stress, including one powerful game Sarah generated on the spot to help her husband at the time deal with mounting pressures. Watch Sarah's creativity in action as you learn how she used laughter for herself and others to cope during the COVID-19 pandemic.

In **Chapter 9,** we outline action steps you can take to begin a successful habit of laughing purposefully and playfully for health and joy. You'll read about Rachael's 40-Day Laughter Challenge, and the declaration she made to become a Laughter Champion. You'll learn how committing to add laughter to her daily routine helped Rachael become more of the playful, positive person she wanted to be. You can choose to modify or duplicate what Rachael did.

Life doesn't only include challenges. **Chapter 10** shows you how to connect with laughter. Rituals and festivities provide moments to pause and acknowledge key life passages. Specific holidays now exist to promote and champion the virtues of laughter. In addition to the laughter holidays, find our *Fun Holidays Calendar* to ignite your creativity. We'll also show you how to add mini laughter celebrations to everyday occurrences. Moments, big and small, can all be infused with laughter.

In **Chapter 11**, we share many of the fascinating fun facts and discoveries that we unearthed during our research. As laughter professionals, we've studied laughter and practiced laughing with people all over the world for nearly two decades. Our collective experience prepared us to expand our vision for a laughter-filled future which you will also find in this chapter.

While we haven't included a full bibliography, we've provided **Additional Resources**, including a treasure trove of books we enjoyed, so you can satisfy your curiosity and delve deeper into areas of particular interest.

As we wrote, we gained important insights worth sharing because they propelled us forward, grabbed our attention, and enhanced our relationship with each other. Writing collaboratively spurred our creativity and led to a lot of shared giggles and side-splitting laughter. The process resulted in a unique collection of lessons and practices to apply, master, and share, both personally and professionally.

Because some of us have a difficult time just letting go and laughing like children, we created a tool called the *Laughter Participation Scale* to help you identify your comfort level with purposeful, playful laughter moment to moment.

You'll learn how to invite your Inner Child out to play and send your Inner Critic to time-out—whether you're resistant

 **LAUGHTER PARTICIPATION SCALE**

 Uninhibited and Free

 Eager

 Engaged

 Willing to Experiment

 Curious

 Cautious

 Skeptical

 Fearful

 Not Interested at All

to laughter or ready to embrace it fully. You'll learn how to lean into laughter when life is weighing you down, and how to celebrate with laughter whenever the opportunity arises. You'll also discover how the practice of laughing purposefully and playfully will ultimately empower you to burst into laughter more often and easily.

We've done a *lot* of research, delving into every aspect of laughter imaginable, poring through myriad studies, articles, and books. Although only a fraction of what we unearthed made its way into this book, all of that information influenced everything we've written. We've sprinkled this book with scientific, cultural, and historical references to give you a better understanding and appreciation of the important roles of laughter and play in our health and well-being, in our relationships with others, and in the world.

Data alone isn't enough. We've identified different skills to help you achieve the goal of sustained belly laughs. Each skill is fun and easy to do on its own. You'll find these pages laced with a variety of tools and techniques to guide you.

You'll notice *Fun Facts* throughout this book, which are items to stimulate your curiosity. By the time you finish reading this book, we want you to have experienced some genuine smiles and become acquainted with the sound of your own laugh. *Speed Bumps* give you an opportunity to pause and take a moment for self-reflection. *Jump Starts* help you ease into sustained belly laughs. *Laughter Breaks* provide you an opportunity to practice aloud while you're reading. Willingly or reluctantly, take the *Laughter Breaks* and do the *Jump Starts* to start having fun. You can revisit these laughter-generating tools as a way to share what you've learned and to enhance your own self-care.

Why This Book?

The "why" behind *Discover the Power of Laughter* is simple: When it comes to health and well-being, the more laughter the better. Millions of people are suffering from chronic stress, which can degrade health and quality of life. Laughter is free, fun, and portable. Laughter neutralizes stress hormones as it boosts immunity. Virtually anyone can develop and sustain a life-long, joy-enhancing laughter practice.

Use the book to add more laughter to your life, whether you are alone, with a friend, or in a group. Keep it as a guide and share it. Mastery comes from regularly practicing hearty laughter, sharing the ideas and games, and encouraging others to laugh along with you.

Our journey begins with Sarah's story.

"Life is 10% what happens to you and 90% how you respond."

Irving Berlin, Composer

One

Sarah's Story: Choosing to Laugh

When I was seven, I made a conscious choice to laugh through life as a tribute to my Grandpa Barney. For as long as I can remember, I've loved hearing the story of Grandpa's reaction to my birth. I was the unexpected second twin, coined by my mother as her Bonus Baby. When my grandfather learned there were two of us, he let loose with a big "YIPPEE!" on the phone. No wonder I loved him so fiercely. I felt his warmth and jovial demeanor even before we met. Every time I saw him, he greeted me with a huge grin that burst into shared spontaneous laughter.

Because our grandparents lived only an hour away, they visited us regularly. Often Grandpa Barney walked Rachael and me to school. One day, during second grade, Grandpa Barney walked us only half-way. I remember exactly where we stood when he stopped, on Elsmere Avenue, on the driveway, near the end of the street. I felt his grip on my hand ease as he turned to us and said, "This is as far as I'm going to go, girls." I begged and pleaded with him to walk us the whole way. He quietly said, "No, this is as far as I'm going to go today." His refusal surprised me. I didn't understand why he wouldn't keep walking as he usually did. The lump in my throat grew as I thought about him with sadness and confusion for the rest of the walk to school.

Three days later, just before our seventh birthday, Grandpa Barney died of a sudden heart attack. I looked for signs of him everywhere but found nothing—no laugh, no hug. I missed the comfort of being with him. I felt cold and numb. I didn't even cry. I knew Grandpa Barney loved me and wanted me to be happy and filled with joy. I thought I couldn't feel him near me because I was too filled with sadness.

Right then, at age seven, I decided I would become the happiest person I could be, for him, and then I would always feel Grandpa Barney's presence.

My choice to be like Grandpa and respond to life with smiles and laughter was soon tested. During second grade I had to wear an eye patch to strengthen my weak eye and prevent eye surgery. I tried not to think about it until one summer day when I went to the swimming pool with my twin sister, Rachael, our five-year-old sister, Julie, and our nine-year-old cousin, Phyllis. While we were playing, a group of kids snickered at me and pointed in my direction.

Were they making fun of me? I wanted to melt into the concrete or dive into the water and not come up for a really long time. I thought about Grandpa and how fun and funny he was. I knew if he were here, he'd know exactly what to do. He would find a way to get me laughing right now. I glanced toward the kids, turned back to my sisters and cousin, grabbed their hands, and laughed as I led them away. Grandpa would be so proud.

I also decided that people would only see the free-spirited, happy me, never the vulnerable, needy me. I buried everything but joyful expression. Whenever I faced a difficult or uncomfortable situation, I couldn't bear to let anyone see that I was secretly insecure and worried about how others saw me. I learned to put on a smile and hoped I was convincing.

When I had to wear a full-bodied back brace during high school, I worked hard to make sure the carefree, fun-loving girl shone so brightly that no one would notice the contraption. If I could control my attitude toward the unsightly brace, I could pretend it didn't exist.

My positive and upbeat response to life during tough times served me well, and I expected this strategy would continue to protect me, even when my youngest child, Jacqueline, became very ill.

Jacqueline's health issues first introduced themselves on the sixth day of her life when she stopped breathing. That began our many hospital visits and stays. Months later, we learned she had multiple serious health issues, many related to an underlying immune deficiency disease.

When she was eight months old, my husband Brent stayed home with our daughters Allison, five, and Monica, two, while I lived with Jacqueline in the hospital in North Carolina, a five-hour drive from our home in Georgia. Jacqueline eventually received two bone marrow transplants from Monica, whose bone marrow was a perfect match.

Beeping machines and worries about our struggling little girl kept me up at night. I was facing my most difficult challenge yet. Presenting a joyful countenance required keeping the pain to myself.

I believe positivity breeds good things, and physical surroundings impact our attitudes. To brighten our temporary home, Rachael helped me hang a shower curtain with vivid colorful fish. We bought a polka dot futon and placed it in the bathroom where it became my bed and doubled as Jacqueline's play space. Colorful posters and cheery sayings dotted the hospital walls. The rainbow-colored *I Love You Very Much* poster was the focus. Bright colors reached out and warmed me like a giant hug. Whenever I saw the words, I tried to convince myself that if I could pour as much love into Jacqueline as Grandpa Barney had poured into me, I could keep her safe.

Intent on creating a positive lively experience for both of us every day, I distracted myself with art projects while Jacqueline looked on, tracking my every move.

Jacqueline's numerous health challenges and my deep desire to protect her kept me on high alert, while she stayed busy being a typical baby: curious, interested, quick to laugh. Her wonder and joy were palpable. Her light-heartedness was exactly what I needed to help me relax.

Just outside Jacqueline's room was a special closed-off area with a sink and soap for hand scrubbing. It also housed a ready supply of sterile gloves, gowns, masks, and shoe and hair coverings. To protect Jacqueline from outside germs, doctors, nurses, and visitors who entered her room had to follow the antiseptic protocol to protect her from infections. When Allison and Monica came to visit, they were given fresh new clothes to put on. Dressed in their new outfits, with freshly scrubbed hands, they were eager to visit their baby sister. As immediate family members, they didn't have to wear masks.

Whenever Brent visited, Jacqueline perked up—she looked at her father through the glass door and smiled from her crib as she waited eagerly for him to change into clean clothes so he could enter her world. She became more animated as she reached for him and the long-awaited daddy-embrace. Once he entered the room, the two of them were like hugging magnets.

During one visit Brent held Jacqueline on his lap and pointed to the colorful poster. He read each word aloud, "I . . . Love . . . " and when he got to the word "YOU," he squeezed her with a delicious tickle and giggle. She squealed with laughter that I can almost hear as I write this. Her father caught the giggles. When I heard my own voice laughing out loud, I realized I had caught the giggles, too! Peals of our laughter swirled around the room. I heard Brent's drawn-out laughter laced with Jacqueline's playful giggles and snorts, along with my own unrestrained laughter.

The shared laughter rose like a crescendo filling the room. I sensed a shift in the air and inside me. Momentarily, I forgot where we were.

Distinct from Jacqueline's usual playful laughter, these snorts and giggles went deeper. *Just be with me,* her entire demeanor insisted. Jacqueline's giggles expanded, became hypnotic, and like the Pied Piper, compelled us to follow. The sterile walls of her hospital room transformed into the imaginary place of fairies vividly described in the daily stories I told her and shared with her sisters in letters and on the phone. Her laughter transported us to the twisted roots of the ginkgo tree that guarded the entrance to the garden we visited when we could get outside. We hung our worries on the tree to fly away with the gentle breeze. Suddenly, we were in the magical land of unbridled laughter and unfettered joy.

Was I imagining this? I felt like skipping. Without any advance warning or decision on my part, our sad and critical situation shifted. I pictured us a happy family again—Allison and Monica playing with us, their chuckles and carefree laughter encircling ours. The burden of separation and unknown medical outcomes temporarily disappeared.

For the first time in months, I relaxed fully, and a peaceful smile arose on my face. I felt renewed and lighter in my entire body, as if I were floating. A huge, heavy weight had been lifted. I never realized uninhibited laughter held so much power. The experience changed me. I felt more determined than ever to savor each moment with Jacqueline. The gift of this shared laughter experience deepened my understanding and commitment to mindfulness. Finding the most joy I could in each moment became a heightened priority.

Jacqueline was gone before her second birthday.

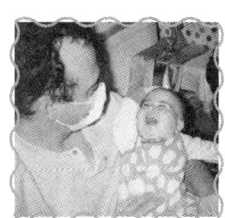  

Our happy family of three beautiful girls suddenly felt very small. I loved Allison and Monica deeply, but with Jacqueline gone, a gaping hole sat with all of us, every day. Allison could still be a big sister to Monica, but Monica no longer had a younger sister who looked up to her. She gravitated to younger children, and I watched in amazement as she played with them with a protective air.

I've come to understand grief is a very personal experience. Each of us has a unique timeline and way to process and integrate the loss. In the year following Jacqueline's death, I spent a lot of time digging in the garden. I often relived my time with her in the hospital as I pored over photographs, but I couldn't regenerate her joy and her laughter. Now, in addition to missing Grandpa Barney's spirit, I also longed to be surrounded by Jacqueline's joyful giggles. Brent couldn't even look at photographs of her or talk about the good times. For him, the loss was too painful.

In kindergarten, in a new school in a new state, Monica told everyone she met that she had a baby sister who had died. Allison found it too difficult and complicated to talk about Jacqueline. Like me, she was private and kept most of her feelings inside. As a third grader, when asked how many siblings she had, she answered, "Just one."

As time went on, however, we were able to find fun again as a family. The girls remembered teaching Jacquline to snort while she was home in between bone marrow transplants. Reenacting these snorts provided much needed unbridled laughter. Infusing the emptiness with joyful memories and sounds helped us heal.

Years later, during Allison's first year of college, her friend, Molly invited me to attend a Laughter Yoga session she would be leading. Laughter Yoga is a health-promoting activity often practiced in a group. It combines movement, deep breathing, and intentional laughter. You may be picturing Downward Dog on a yoga mat, but in Laughter Yoga the focus is on imagination and play. No humor or yoga mat is required. I would be laughing in a room with a bunch of strangers. I had no idea what to expect, but I went because Molly asked me. I arrived with the intention to participate fully.

I had never been instructed to simply laugh out loud. I looked around the room. Sure. I'll laugh along. But how? We all shrugged our shoulders in silent agreement—we'd go along despite our lack of understanding and muddle through the best we could. I was sure I could eke out a small chuckle to prove I was fully present. The awkward sound I heard coming from my own throat was barely audible and without feeling.

Molly had us promise to be kind to each other and not judge ourselves or anyone else as she instructed us in the laughter exercises. Immediately, as she began, her enthusiastic robust laughter filled the room. She successfully teased giggles out of us. Self-conscious, I pretended she was dressed as a ballerina flitting around the room, and I managed to let out a chuckle or two. Then, to my surprise, I genuinely laughed. I wondered what others were imagining. Maybe they pictured her in a more outlandish way. As people became engaged in the playful laughter exercises, something remarkable happened: I began to laugh freely.

I noticed my uncomfortable half-giggles had become easy, prolonged bursts of laughter. I was no longer pretending, but laughing from somewhere deep inside. The same thing was happening throughout the room: spontaneous, full-bodied laughter, not forced or fake. I was mystified. As further instructed, we were making eye contact with each other. As a result, the room escalated into unstoppable boisterous sounds of joy. I was enveloped and uplifted. I wasn't the only one—everyone genuinely laughed. The more I heard others laugh, the deeper my own laughter became. I felt myself letting go completely. Time melted away.

What just happened? I felt liberated after laughing on cue with total strangers!

Afterward, as I walked to my car, I realized laughing with the group recreated what I longed for: the magic of laughter—the feelings of joy laced with the love, connection, and contentment I had felt when laughing with Jacqueline and Brent in the hospital.

If a single 45-minute Laughter Yoga session could tear down my carefully guarded walls of protection, generate a gush of light-heartedness, and bring me fully into the present moment, I knew I had to learn and share this practice.

In Laughter Yoga, deliberate laughter quickly becomes authentic. Unlike most reactions to humor, Laughter Yoga is a practice of sustained laughter and that is when the magic happens.

The practice of Laughter Yoga empowers me to choose to laugh whenever I need it. The more I laugh, the more comfortable I am in my own skin. Laughing out loud with others helps me unwind as I feel more grounded and connected.

I like to say Laughter Yoga is heavy on laughter and light on yoga. We don't use mats in Laughter Yoga. No special clothing. No funky positions. And no *om*. Like yoga, we do pay attention to deep diaphragmatic breathing.

In the months following my first session with Molly, I became certified as a Laughter Yoga leader, and several years later became a trainer. In the decades since, I have been fulfilling my vision to spread the power and possibility of intentional laughter with others. As I teach people to laugh deliberately, and speak of the myriad benefits of hearty laughter, I continue to discover that purposeful laughter makes a profound difference for so many.

For example, a man, who had laughed with me for a mere twenty minutes, told me that since attending my laughter session a year earlier, he and his young daughter enthusiastically start every day with shared smiles and giggles. A college student shared that after he left an hour-long laughter session his headache and sore throat were gone. To see the changes in people's faces, to feel the energy shift in the room, and to learn the positive impact purposeful laughter often has on people's lives inspires me to laugh more in my own life.

FUN FACT

Jokes Turn into Play

When Dr. Madan Kataria started Laughter Yoga in 1995, in Mumbai, India, he gathered people in the park to laugh. He had been researching an article for his health magazine and came across a man who had reportedly cured a very perilous condition with laughter. The story ignited the idea of a laughter club, and he immediately took action to create one. When the jokes he told to the gathered people started to get stale, he asked for twenty-four hours and promised the next day they'd laugh without jokes. Pulling from some of his research and his love of theater he created laughter exercises that involved acting out common activities, like making a milkshake. He infused the actions with imagination and play and stimulated people to laugh. The contagious nature of laughter helped him succeed. He added deep yogic breathing and Laughter Yoga was born.

Soon after my daughters graduated college and grad school, they learned their father and I were getting divorced. I hated that they would have to endure another big loss.

Their solution? An adventure road trip! *En-Rout: Miles of Smiles* became a volunteer tour around the United States to spread health and happiness. They taught oral health to children at Boys and Girls Clubs and offered Laughter Yoga to some of the people who needed it most—families at Ronald McDonald House Charities, where we had stayed when Jacqueline was receiving treatment. They asked me to certify them as Laughter Yoga Leaders before they left. I was excited to be able to contribute. I knew it would be a powerful tool for them. They spent 110 days driving through 41 states with 16 volunteer stops along the way. Their focus on smiles and laughter contributed significantly to their own healing.

JUMP START

De-Stress with Grins and Giggles

When you want to stop feeling so much *stress*... smile, even if you don't feel like it. Take a few deep breaths, and giggle as you exhale. Be on the lookout for any resistance.

How'd it go?

Oh... notice any hesitation?

Every person's journey with laughter is different. Until the writing of this book, I hadn't thought much about it. We all find different coping mechanisms to help us through the rough spots. I had used laughter to my advantage many times. I never stopped to consider there are people who struggle with their very relationship with laughter, even though I had spent a good part of my life living with someone who had done just that.

I'd like to introduce you to my twin sister, Rachael, so she can tell you her story.

"Laughter gives us distance. It allows us to step back from an event, deal with it, and then move on."

Bob Newhart, Comedian

Two

Rachael's Story: Choosing *Not* to Laugh

Until I was nine years old, I knew who I was. I was the identical twin of my sister Sarah, and I was happy.

A big change occurred the day we went to a bowling birthday party. Several girls we didn't know stood us back-to-back and pointed out as many differences between us as they could, like the scar on my forehead versus the scar on Sarah's chin. As usual, they were looking for ways to figure out who was who. Being compared so closely never bothered me. I enjoyed the feeling that I was part of something unique and special. On the way home from the party, one of the girls asked me, "How do you tell yourself apart from your sister?" My jaw dropped. I didn't know how to respond. Was she actually asking me how I knew I was me, and not Sarah?

How do you tell yourself apart from someone else? Do you look in the mirror and measure your height and ponytails? I sat in silence as the enormity of her question shattered my sense of self, because I had always defined myself as a twin.

What made Me, Me?

What made Sarah, Sarah?

For as long as I can remember, I have processed my life through the twin lens. Sarah was someone who boldly asserted her independence. She seemed oblivious to what anyone thought about her. She carved her own path whenever possible. I thought we shared a built-in, unspoken, intimate relationship. She clung to her privacy. When she was unhappy, she didn't even let me know.

In contrast, I saw myself as *inter*dependent. I shared almost *everything* with Sarah. So, I was shocked when, as an adult, she shared with me that she never thought of herself as being defined by me at all. Sarah was outgoing, laughed, and made friends easily. She was her own person. It finally made sense to me why I came to feel like her shadow. Somewhere deep inside, I felt I was slowly losing part of myself. Growing up, I became focused, serious, and intentional—all fairly opposite of Sarah's personality traits.

Sarah spent a lot of our childhood defending my moodiness to other people. I felt eternally grateful. She repeatedly encouraged me to feel better about myself and tried to boost my mood. I remember recurring conversations about me smiling more. One incident stands out, and we both recall the exact conversation. I was in one of my funks. Sarah marched me to a mirror and forced me to look at our reflections. Smiling into the mirror, she asked, "What do you see?"

"You're beautiful," I said.

"We're identical twins," she said. "We look exactly alike! If I'm beautiful, you are beautiful."

"But I'm ugly," I whispered.

"Don't you dare call me ugly!" Sarah said. She made silly faces until I started to giggle. Finally, when we were both laughing, Sarah said, "Now, don't you see, we're *both* beautiful?"

Reluctantly, I had to agree. But even Sarah's loving nudges didn't stop me from feeling fundamentally unhappy. I remember how I used to beg Sarah to trade birthday presents with me, even before we opened them. I viewed everything she had as better. I continually compared myself to her—and usually I came up short. I wanted to be her until we were in our twenties.

Sarah was able to roll with the punches and laugh things off, even in difficult or challenging situations, like when she lost the seventh grade student council election, didn't win the speech contest, and when she had to wear an ugly back brace in high school. When I made mistakes or did something embarrassing, I cried in the bathroom, got an upset stomach, or walked around with my head down for the rest of the day. Would I ever be able to find joyful self-expression like Sarah? It seemed I was doomed—especially after what happened on a family trip to Disneyland during the summer after fourth grade.

After deliriously laughing through the last big drop on Disneyland's most popular new roller coaster ride, the giant Matterhorn, I felt a warm, wet sensation fill my seat. Little did I know, I had just experienced stress incontinence. I like to call it tension-easer pee. It's caused by the contraction of the detrusor muscle around the bladder during laughter, in case you were wondering (maybe you've experienced it—many people do).

As the ride stopped, so did my fun. Bars sprang open. With just seconds to jump out, I was too mortified to warn an adult. The next poor soul hopped into my pee puddle. I didn't stick around to see what happened. Terrible thoughts swarmed; I had peed through my favorite shorts outfit, which I'd sewn myself. I urgently found a bathroom where I washed my shorts and dried them with the electric hand dryer. I avoided answering my mother's concerned question about what took me so long in the bathroom. I told no one, not even Sarah. I felt so stigmatized, as if I had been branded. For the rest of the day a cloud of shame hovered over me, and I hoped no one else could perceive my embarrassment and disgrace. I spent the next thirteen hours with family at the Magic Kingdom feeling self-conscious, ashamed, and nervous. I couldn't, *wouldn't*, risk another laughter "accident." *So much for the happiest place on earth.*

Better not take any risks.

No more surprises.

Those uncompromising directives from my Inner Critic continued to remind me that fun was precarious.

That day at Disneyland, my Inner Child took a back seat and my Inner Critic started running my life. As we left the bright lights of Main Street that night, I made a solemn promise to myself that I would never lose control again.

In seventh grade, I remember being extremely frustrated during science lab. My teacher, Mrs. Dillon, privately offered some advice. She said, "One of the most important lessons you will discover in life is to learn to laugh at yourself. The sooner you learn it, the happier you will be."

Whoa, do people actually laugh at themselves? Could I learn to laugh at myself?

Her words stuck with me. Laughing at myself when I goofed up seemed like a good idea. But as I thought about Sarah and her eye patch at the swimming pool, I believed laughing at myself was like those kids laughing at Sarah—mocking and humiliating. I was not going to mock myself!

That left me with a dilemma: Laughing more and taking life in stride is a good idea. *How do I take myself and life less seriously and still keep everything under control?*

I couldn't figure it out. Instead of becoming more lighthearted, I focused intensely on doing excellent schoolwork and becoming a leader in my youth group. I was a perfectionist. I was not going to laugh at myself—I saw that as cruel. Still, I wanted to be known for something, like Sarah was known as fun and spontaneous. Being identified as serious was fine with me until people mistook my intensity for unhappiness.

For the next few years, I was comfortable in my role as the serious twin. And then, I embarrassed myself with laughter again in tenth grade. We had two phones in our house, one upstairs, one down. The phone rang and I picked up the upstairs extension as I heard my father solemnly telling my mother, who was downstairs, "Grandma Dina just died."

I hung up the phone as quickly as I could so they wouldn't know I had been on the extension. My throat tensed and suddenly . . . I was laughing. I was mortified! It was awful! I couldn't *stop* laughing.

Sarah asked, "What's so funny?"

In between my uncontrollable chortles, I managed to let out the words. "Grandma Dina . . . just . . . died." But not without several more guffaws.

Sarah shouted at me, "What's wrong with you? That's not funny!"

Our other sister, Julie, was yelling at me, too, "Stop laughing! What's the matter with you?"

I knew Grandma Dina's death wasn't funny. Losing her didn't feel funny to me either. I was ashamed and embarrassed. But I kept right on laughing—trying desperately but failing to stuff down the morbid sounds coming from my throat. The more they criticized the laughing the worse I felt and the harder I laughed. My self-loathing grew. I saw myself as the serious twin, the one who rarely laughed . . . until somebody *died*!

While I had no control of or explanation for my inappropriate burst of laughter, I had no problem slipping into self-judgment and self-loathing. My Inner Critic was having a heyday! I wasn't very happy with myself, and I had failed again to maintain my composure.

FUN FACT

Nervous Laughter

When you find yourself having an incongruous emotion that results in an uncontrollable fit of laughter, no need to worry. It's a physical release, called *nervous laughter*— your body's signal that you have experienced extreme stress, shock, or trauma. Laughing at an awkward moment is your body trying to restore you to balance. Sometimes it backfires—you actually feel more tension after laughing than before. If you find yourself laughing inappropriately, you can use the embarrassing moment as an opportunity to let people know that laughing is your way to release tension, and not an indication of amusement.

Nervous laughter runs in our family. During high school, a bird flew into our house through the chimney. It was flying around the living room. Our father donned a trench coat, heavy gloves, and a large hat. Armed with a broom and a brown paper bag, he frantically ran around trying to catch the bird so it wouldn't harm anyone or escape into any other part of the house. My sisters and I were too scared to notice how ridiculous our father looked. In the midst of all the commotion our mother walked through the front door. Seeing her husband dressed like that while waving his hands in the air, she began to laugh hysterically. She couldn't believe her eyes and wondered what could possibly be going on. We yelled over her laughter that there was a bird flying around the house. Dad got very angry and annoyed at her laughter. He confessed later, that he felt scared, though he tried to put on a brave face for us. The more upset he grew, the more robust mom's laughter became. Years later she told us of her anxiety and fear in that moment. She hadn't thought anything was funny. She was scared. He thought she was laughing *at him*. They never talked about it. Apparently, they didn't know about *nervous laughter,* either. The bird had the last laugh and flew out safely.

Nervous laughter is our body's way of protecting us. Without understanding that, it's no wonder I was filled with so much self-loathing for not having kept my emotions in check. My constant negative self-judgment likely contributed to my trip to the emergency room when I was sixteen. I was diagnosed with Crohn's Disease and hospitalized for a month. Perhaps lightening up would have been good, as Mrs. Dillon had suggested.

The doctor gave me two instructions: avoid stress and don't keep emotions buried inside. No one gave me the slightest hints about how to attain stress relief. And I didn't ask. I was afraid I would look stupid, and anyway, how could I avoid stress as I prepared to leave home, go to college, and then law school? I diligently took the prescribed medicine and strictly adhered to the restrictive diet I was given. I also became extremely successful at wearing my emotions on my sleeve. The doctor had given me a huge permission slip to express myself. All my stress spilled out in the form of negativity.

At that point my Inner Critic was running the show with all the weapons needed to kill off the possibility of any laughter. I felt I had permission to be solemn. No one could shame me for being studious, determined, and conscientious.

Sarah continued to be a cheerleader for me into adulthood, especially when encouraging positivity. Even during Jacqueline's illness, she continued to check in with me to make sure I was okay and staying upbeat throughout my own challenges. After she became a Laughter Yoga leader, some of our phone calls became mini laughter sessions. As I learned about the value of vigorous laughter and then directly experienced it for myself, I started sharing Sarah's work with others and became her cheerleader. At the same time, I started to revisit my early choice not to laugh. My relationship with laughter was evolving.

As I worked with Sarah in developing her business, laughter became more familiar and comfortable to me. Then, an experience in my own kitchen caused me to reconsider laughter with keener interest. While preparing a meal for a large group of people, tensions began to mount. I turned into the kitchen drill sergeant, delegating tasks to each family member. My reputation as a good hostess on the line, I felt impatient and prodded people to move faster. My husband didn't want to be in the line of fire, so he tiptoed past me. Tension hung in the air.

A few weeks prior to this, Sarah had led our family in a Laughter Yoga session. Recalling one of the *Laughter Games* Sarah had taught us, my oldest daughter, Rina, used it on the spot. She shifted the stress-filled energy into playfulness, and we all started laughing. It was difficult to ignore the laughter session as the source of that transformation.

Soon after, I asked Sarah to train me as a Laughter Yoga leader even though I didn't expect to lead laughter sessions. I wanted to learn how to add more laughter to my life without resorting to humor, especially since I had little appreciation for most things others found funny.

In the intimate safe space of the Laughter Yoga training, my deep-seated inhibitions toward laughter began to melt away. My friend Bev was demonstrating her new dancing laughter game and I literally jumped up to dance with her as we laughed uncontrollably. When we paused long enough to breathe, I noticed I was fully present and having fun. I was excited to re-discover my sense of play. I wondered if I would be able to let go like this again.

It's been more than nine years since I danced with Bev the first time. I can confirm, indeed, I can and did let go, again and again.

While writing this book, I drew a *Laughter Participation Scale* to help me visualize how I felt in any given moment about laughing out loud. Seeing the different faces with their labels allowed me to look at what was holding me back and identify what it might take to move up the scale. It became like a game for me.

LAUGHTER BREAK

 # Laugh Out Loud

It's time to laugh out loud again.
Right now.

Go ahead...
Take a deep breath, and
Say, *Ha-Ha-Ha*!
Louder. *HA-HA-HA*!

So, was that easier than the first time we invited you?
Did you actually do it?
Did you get a good chuckle out of it?

Consider the *Laughter Participation Scale* on this page and then locate yourself on it. Sarah started out at the very top, *Uninhibited and Free*. I started at the bottom, *Not Interested at All*. Make a note for yourself where you are on the scale in this moment. You may find yourself going up and down the scale and skipping levels repeatedly, and that's okay! If you are reluctant to accept our invitations to laugh out loud, you may be holding onto some resistance.

LAUGHTER PARTICIPATION SCALE

 Uninhibited and Free

 Eager

 Engaged

 Willing to Experiment

 Curious

 Cautious

 Skeptical

 Fearful

 Not Interested at All

Let's Talk About Resistance

Resistance is easy to spot. When it's time to laugh—you don't. You're not a child, and you think you're above all that silliness. You want to be respected and taken seriously. Or maybe fear of embarrassment and humiliation arise inside you, creating a powerful shield that you hope will prevent you from sounding weird, looking foolish, or losing control. Even if you have a well-behaved detrusor muscle and aren't worried about creating pee puddles when you laugh, you may still choose to suppress laughter when you have a deep desire to fit in. You may seek to avoid social discomfort in response to the pleadings of your Inner Critic. Full self-expression eludes you.

> **FEARS THAT TRIGGER RESISTANCE**
>
> Fear of being judged, ridiculed, or laughed at.
> Fear of appearing phoney, fake, childish, or immature.
> Fear of incontinence. Fear of sounding
> weird or looking unattractive.

> **DESIRES THAT TRIGGER RESISTANCE**
>
> Desire to be authentic and accepted.
> Desire to be respected and taken seriously.
> Desire to maintain control and fit in.

> **BELIEFS THAT TRIGGER RESISTANCE**
>
> Laughter is a luxury I don't have time to indulge in.
> I'm feeling depressed and not joyful at all.
> I don't see what's so funny. It's not right to laugh at others.

Another way to think about resistance is to picture speed bumps. Some speed bumps are invisible. You may have encountered a few already while reading. Did you get bored, want to put the book down, or resist our invitations to participate in the *Jump Starts* we created to help you warm up? Those pauses in interest or participation may be clues to alert you to a blind spot—an emotional trigger bubbling up from your laughter memories. They might take the form of silent conversations in your head, *Everyone else is laughing. Nothing's even **funny**— why are people laughing? Is there something wrong with **me**?* Something inside you has decided not to laugh and you feel stuck. You may encounter speed bumps to laughter almost anywhere. If you ignore them, over the years they can create a deep-seated unconscious pattern of resistance, like what happened to me.

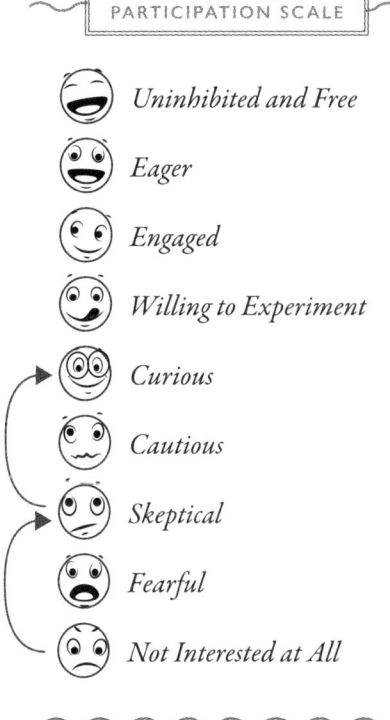

What If I'm Not Ready?

We've created some useful visual *Speed Bumps* for you throughout this book. Each *Speed Bump* is an invitation to pause and do a quick self-assessment before you continue reading. We hope these pauses will help you choose to accelerate up the *Laughter Participation Scale.* You may find it helpful to hold your Inner Child on your lap and reassure the Cautious You that it's safe to come out to play.

In my case, once I began doing research for several laughter projects Sarah was working on, including this book, I made some fascinating discoveries that caused me to move from *Not Interested at All* through *Skeptical* and into *Curious.*

SPEED BUMP

Have You Met Your Inner Critic?

How loud is your Inner Critic? Do you even notice that soft whisper of self-doubt whenever a challenging social situation arises? It could be directly critical or cause you to speak sarcastically, defensively, or to not speak at all.

An easy way to separate the voice of the Inner Critic from your desire to be joyful and self-expressed, is to simply chuckle. You can smile, grin, or chuckle with recognition whenever you start to notice that little negative voice in your head.

Think about whether this is a *Speed Bump* or a *Jump Start* for you. When your Inner Critic is loud and you are *Not Interested at All* in laughing, what will it take to get you past *Fearful*, *Skeptical*, and *Cautious*, up to *Curious*, or even *Willing*? Be brave as you knock down your own resistance one chuckle at a time.

Aware of the myriad benefits of robust laughter, it's hard for Sarah to understand why everyone wouldn't dive right in and join this often-overlooked path to wellness. When she pauses and thinks about my resistance, she remembers that not everyone has the same easy path to laughter.

FUN FACT

Gelatophobics

Did you know, there is actually a word for someone who is pathologically afraid of being laughed at? *Gelotophobics* suffer from a fear of being laughed at and can't stand to hear chuckles since they believe they are the butt of the joke. *Gelotophobia* can be caused by past trauma, parents, culture, bullying, or social anxiety.

Travel at your own pace. If you're still aware of some resistance to expressing full-bodied laughter without humor, courageously invite your inquisitive Inner Child out to explore. A fun formula and tools await you.

"Laughter puts your brain, your central nervous system and your whole being into a state of free play."

Max Eastman, Author

Three

Ready or Not, Laugh!

There's more to Disneyland than yellow snow on the Matterhorn. On the same day of Rachael's Matterhorn incident, as Disneyland was slowly closing for the day, our cousins noticed that the kiddie train ride was still open and scrambled aboard determined to prolong the day's merriment. A tiny bump in the track passed for a four-year-old's imitation of a roller-coaster.

Our twelve-year-old cousin Peggy had a distinctive and extremely contagious laugh resembling a mating call of the exotic birds in the Enchanted Tiki Room. As the kiddie train took off and slowly rounded a corner, Peggy put her hands up in the air and roared with tropical bird laughter, generating unrestrained fun for those of us riding the train as well as the on-lookers. Peggy unknowingly demonstrated how to trigger and enjoy random outbursts of laughter—without humor. Even *Rachael* caught Peggy's infectious laughter and chuckled out loud.

Most people can't generate enthusiastic laughter from thin air like Peggy did. We envy the few who can, those with magnetic personalities who are the life of the party. You, too, have access to Peggy's power of playfulness. Like Dorothy tapping her ruby red slippers, we created a formula to empower your ability to conjure laughter at will.

We call it Anatomy of a Laugh: Smile ~ Breathe ~ Play

Smile—
Your Access to Laughter

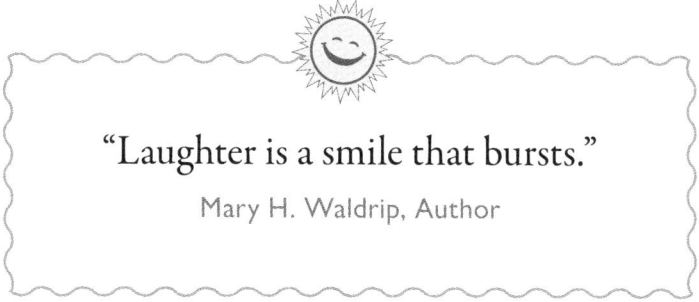

> "Laughter is a smile that bursts."
>
> Mary H. Waldrip, Author

Smiling is the prelude to laughter. Smiling enables people to safely lower their defenses, often hidden behind walls of etiquette, pretense, and fear, and to gently enter the inner sanctum of laughter.

We're here to escort you in.

Watch a person laughing, and the first thing you'll see is a smile. Smiling creates endorphins and gets your body chemistry heading in the correct direction—away from stress, toward joyful energy.

Smile-Ups— The Gateway to Laughter

While leading one of her early Laughter Yoga sessions, Sarah noticed some of her participants appeared uncomfortable and hesitant. To encourage them to shed their reservations and start laughing, she told them not to laugh. She thought to herself, *Even a shy person can feel confident returning a smile without feeling weird or self-conscious.* Then, she said, "Smile! Do it again. A little bit bigger. Expand your smile from ear to ear. Let joy bubble up from inside you." Many of them eagerly participated. Sarah detected some awkward giggling as some people started to loosen up. Soon the giggles became chuckles and gradually transformed into genuine contagious laughter.

Sarah only intended to help the participants prepare their face muscles for hearty laughter by having them smile first. She stumbled upon an effortless way to usher people into genuine laughter. To her delight and surprise, Smile-Ups were born!

FUN FACT

Duchenne Smile

The smile of pure enjoyment—known as the *Duchenne smile,* named for the man who described it—is the one most associated with feelings of true happiness. This "genuine" smile engages your lips and cheeks and causes the corners of your eyes to crinkle. A genuine smile sends endorphins to the brain, blocking the production of the stress hormone, cortisol. Smiling disarms your resistance, creates comfort, and generates instant connection between strangers.

For the folks in Sarah's laughter classes, smiles are the gateway to the ultimate goal, laughter. Sarah now starts her laughter sessions with some form of Smile-Ups.

LAUGHTER GAME

Smile-Ups

1. Stretch your cheek muscles as you turn your lips up at the corners. You're smiling! You might let out a giggle.
2. Put your attention on cheerful things to increase your chances of producing a genuine *Duchenne smile.*
3. Let your eyes dance—crinkle them at the outside corners.
4. Hold the smile for a few seconds.
5. Relax your face. Loosen your cheek muscles. Calm your eyebrows.
6. Smile again, hold for a few seconds, let go and relax your beautiful face.
7. Repeat 10X for a complete warm-up.

Smile-Ups act as a warm-up and move you from uncertainty toward the easy expression of laughter. You don't have to feel happy to smile. In fact, the perfect time for a Smile-Up is when life is *not* going your way.

Sarah's friend Julie, a nurse, had little faith in the surprising power of smiling until she found herself feeling despondent and overwhelmed by her husband's cancer diagnosis. Julie and Sarah had a conversation about easing into laughter with Smile-Ups. A few days later, on her way to work, Julie noticed her normal ability to stay positive wavering. She played with Smile-Ups as she drove. She laughed the rest of the day as she pictured the way other drivers had looked at her repeated Smile-Ups. Even now when Julie recalls that day, she can't wipe the grin off her face.

Smile-Ups are doubly fun and effective with a Smile Buddy! To raise your chance of success, invite someone else to join you. If you don't have a handy partner, here are some alternatives to a Smile Buddy:

- Smile at your reflection in a mirror.
- Smile at your pet, plant, or stuffed animal.
- Draw smiling faces on your fingers and smile at them. (We've got finger puppets.)
- Imagine your favorite person smiling back at you.

Ready to smile with your Smile Buddy? Do ten Smile-Ups as you face each other or your mirror:

Smile. Relax. Smile. Relax. Smile. Relax. Smile. Relax. Smile. Relax. You've got it. Keep going until you've smiled and relaxed ten times.

Do you feel silly? That's okay. Do more Smile-Ups. The more you smile and laugh, the easier it becomes to smile and laugh on purpose, without the aid of humor.

Keep Smiling Cards

Intentionally sharing smiles can be particularly effective. One day, Rachael's son Levi came home from high school and gave her a card that said, *Keep Smiling.* It was cute. She smiled. Then he invited her to turn it over where she read about the value of a smile.

The card was created by Barry Shore, who contracted a virus in 2004 and became a quadriplegic overnight. Since 2006, Shore has committed to giving away ten million *Keep Smiling* cards. He's already distributed over two and a half million cards in twenty-seven languages. Barry attributes his partial recovery and improved physical condition to his positive attitude, which he boosted by his commitment to sharing smiles around the world. Each card is a gift accompanied by a genuine smile, and often leads to new friendships, shared smiles, and shared laughter.

When Sarah heard about the cards, she began using them as the prelude to introducing Smile-Ups in her laughter sessions. Smiling not only warms you up for laughter, it's also effective for dispelling doom and gloom. Smiling reduces anger and stress and energizes both the giver and receiver of the smile. Smiling influences others to see you as more trustworthy and competent. Smiling can even distract you from physical and emotional pain.

Smile and you become more attractive and approachable. It's the reason Rachael thought Sarah was more beautiful. Even though Rachael and Sarah look alike, Sarah's the one who smiled easily.

Keep Smile-Ups Handy

Think about something annoying. Next time you're facing one of life's little irritations, remember to smile at it. Even if you don't mean it, smile anyway. For example: if you find yourself running late or stuck in a traffic jam, do a round or two of Smile-Ups. When you are stuck in a dull meeting or a boring conversation create an opportunity to smile at someone. Feeling low on energy? Invite a colleague or friend to share a round of Smile-Ups. Or, take a walk to the mirror and clap your hands vigorously while you smile at the person in the mirror. Smile-Ups work with people of all ages and even with those people who view things differently than you. Before you enter a potentially controversial discussion with someone, prepare yourself by doing a pile of Smile-Ups. Keep a few extra ones handy to insert during your conversation. You may emerge as friends, or at least the conversation is likely to be more amiable when peppered with smiles. Keep in mind, smiling is a valuable go-to skill to have on hand.

Rachael

Responding with a Smile

A few years ago, I heard one of the scariest pieces of news a woman can hear: "There is something suspicious in your breast." During the next two weeks I felt rising fear and anxiety as I awaited the breast biopsy.

The day finally came. Driving to the procedure, I heard Sarah's voice: *You can do Smile-Ups anytime! Any place! I promise, even if you force a smile, you will instantly feel less stress. Smiling can even help you feel happy. You don't have to believe me. Just do it!*

I was filled with apprehension because the family history with breast cancer was not good. I dreaded everything. I was scared about the procedure and hearing the biopsy results. I got lost en route and began to panic. Deciding I had nothing to lose, I eked out a feeble Smile-Up. I thought to myself, *This is ridiculous! It can't possibly work!* As I continued doing Smile-Ups, I was shocked to hear myself giggle out loud. I kept forcing smiles, while imagining endorphins swimming around my nerve endings.

As I arrived, my anxiety lifted a hairsbreadth, and I wondered if perhaps Sarah was right. After circling the lot four times, I parked the car and sighed. My thoughts raced as I entered the building. *I hope this biopsy is nothing. This appointment is taking way too long already. I don't have time for this. I'm busy!* Then I remembered mindfulness helps with nervous tension. Maybe focused breathing with healthy directives would calm me down. *Breathe deeply. Slow down. Stay calm. Life is good.*

No luck.

I wasn't feeling calmer as I directed my body and mind toward greater health. My Inner Critic started judging me again as I felt my anxiety begin to rise. I switched back to Smile-Ups. In that moment, it felt like a good proactive thing to do. For some unexplainable reason, I didn't mind looking silly as I smiled. I gave up caring what I looked like. I was counting on my smiles generating more positive emotions as Sarah had promised.

Eventually, I found myself alone in the exam room. I lay on the table with a giant smile plastered on my face. I couldn't tell anymore if this was a nervous smile or a full-blown smile, but I heard myself chuckle at the absurdity as my lips curved into a smile I wasn't feeling. Suddenly, a serious giggle slipped out—a genuine, tiny laugh. My smiles chased the worry away, and I realized I felt significantly better than I had five minutes earlier.

This was amazing!

I didn't want to be just another procedure. I had a funny notion: *What if I could shift the energy in the room to positively influence the outcome?* Suddenly, the professionals appeared. They were about to begin when I surprised myself, interrupted, and said: "Have you done your Smile-Ups today?"

Where in the world did that voice come from? In the parking lot I'd been a curmudgeon!

In a flash we were all doing Smile-Ups and laughing together. I used Smile-Ups to transform my nerve-wracking hospital procedure into new positive connections with strangers. My Inner Child snuck out, despite my attempts to keep her hidden. Good news or bad news, Smile-Ups help dissipate stress in the moment.

I was lucky; the biopsy was benign. The only thing spreading was laughter.

Note: Even though I was already somewhat familiar with Laughter Yoga and the power of laughing out loud at that time, risk-free smiling was the easiest thing I could do to help myself in a panic. ～

You, too, can train yourself to smile BIGGER and more easily. Have fun. It works. Smiling is the most powerful gesture in the world. As Buddhist monk and author, Thich Nhất Hạnh, said, "Sometimes your joy is the source of your smile, but sometimes your smile can be the source of your joy."

Many people can't help chuckling in the middle of a Smile-Up workout. If you managed to smile and relax, but never made it to giggling, don't worry, you're not alone. Like any other exercise, the more you practice, the easier it becomes. The goal is sustained laughter. To get there we have to move beyond smiles.

Get ready to warm up another part of your body for laughter.

Breathe— The Ins and Outs of Laughter

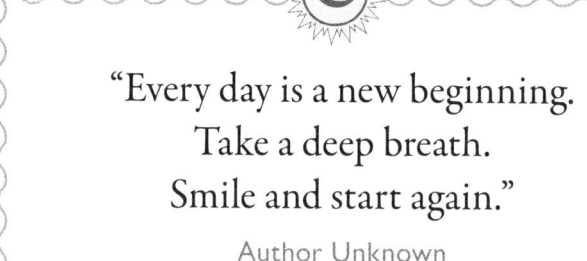

"Every day is a new beginning.
Take a deep breath.
Smile and start again."

Author Unknown

We bet you've never thought of laughter as breathing, but that's exactly what it is, and it is essential to life. Laughter is your body's natural way to increase oxygen flow because laughter, by design, is an exhalation. Put your hand in front of your mouth. Inhale deeply and then, as you exhale, say, *Ha-ha-ha!* Can you feel your breath on your hand? That's a wonderful exhale—congratulations. Do it again, and this time pay careful attention to your diaphragm. Feel it contracting with each sound. The deeper your *Ha* sound, the easier it will be to feel your diaphragm contract.

You can't laugh and inhale at the same time—unless you snort—but we mostly try to avoid that. When you exhale, you're getting rid of carbon dioxide from your lungs, which makes room for more oxygen-rich air to enter with each new breath. We hope you get the picture—the more oxygen you take in, the bigger your laugh can be because you will have more air to exhale.

Deep Belly Breathing

To give yourself the best shot at a successful, long, sustained laugh, we suggest grounding yourself with several conscious deep belly breaths. Healthy babies naturally start out breathing deeply into their abdomens. As many of us grow into adulthood, and life becomes more intense and stressful, we unconsciously shift from the instinctive belly breathing of childhood to more shallow throat breathing. We don't even notice the shift. If you find you've become a shallow breather, it takes just a little practice to get back into the regular habit of deep belly breathing. This kind of breathing is also commonly referred to as abdominal and/or diaphragmatic breathing.

Breath awareness is key to breath control. There are entire books written about it. Things under autonomic control proceed without our awareness, like our heartbeats. Breathing is only partially under autonomic control. Remarkably, we can consciously alter our breathing. We can choose to breathe more slowly, quickly, deeply, shallowly, or even hold our breath. Deep abdominal breathing can be extremely relaxing, and is often taught to pregnant women to assist with pain management and help them rest during childbirth. Regularly practicing deep breathing techniques improves posture, expands your lung capacity, and is key to laughing out loud for extended periods.

Did you find yourself sitting up straight just now?

Warm Up with Laughter Breaths

Are you ready to use your breath to laugh out loud? Rachael developed Laughter Breaths as a way to ease others into laughing on purpose. Sarah uses Laughter Breaths to demonstrate how laughter naturally increases the oxygen flow in the body. Laughter Breaths add sound to your breathing. Don't worry about laughing yet. Laughter Breaths are as easy as Sarah's Smile-Ups. Let's give this tool a try.

JUMP START

Deep Belly Breathing

1. Lie flat on your back, or sit with back straight, shoulders relaxed, and eyes closed.
2. Place your hands on your belly.
3. Breathe in through your nose, paying attention to your stomach as it expands and pushes against your hands.
4. Breathe out through your nose, and notice as your stomach contracts and relaxes.

If you are concerned about your belly poking out as you fill your diaphragm with air, have no fear! You suck your tummy back in when you exhale so it's a temporary bulge.

LAUGHTER GAME

Laughter Breaths

1. Close your mouth and inhale deeply through your nose, filling your lungs with oxygen.

2. As you exhale, open your mouth and slowly vocalize the sound *Ha-Ha-Ha*, over and over again, more and more rapidly. Be on the lookout for a few chuckles to emerge.

3. Do it again, laughing as long as you can.

At some point, hopefully you will feel your inhibitions start to melt and you will catch yourself actually laughing. This is more likely to occur when laughing with a friend or in a group.

4. Continue making *Ha-Ha-Ha* sounds until you need to pause to take another breath. Do it again. Play with the sound, moving it toward the back of your mouth until you feel it tickling your throat and moving down into your chest.

See, you're laughing! Unless you're not. If you're having trouble, and find you're just making noise, carry on, we have other games for you.

5. Complete your Laughter Breaths with *Ha-Ha-Ha* sounds and experiment with *Ho-Ho-Ho* and *He-He-He*. Engage your imagination and allow yourself to have fun. Pay attention to how the shape of your mouth changes with each sound. You can vary the way you laugh by controlling the shape of your lips and pitch of your voice.

Exhaling from the top of your chest creates a high-pitch laugh, while exhaling from the bottom of your belly creates a low-pitch laugh.

Speech and occupational therapists use Laughter Breaths as a fun tool to help children vocalize and engage—turning therapy into a game of laughter. When you coax a smile or laugh from a reluctant child, willing participation and good feelings are sure to follow. Adults hesitant to engage in purposeful laughter will also benefit from the Laughter Breaths game.

As you master Laughter Breaths you'll discover yourself letting go and genuinely laughing as your inhibitions fade. If you are having trouble, engage a friend.

Sarah has laughed for so long that her laughs last a long time. Don't give up. Even if you're breathless after a minute, your diaphragm will become stronger over time. Keep practicing.

Take tiny breaths when you need them—passing out is not part of laughter. Rachael can rarely laugh for a full fifteen seconds without taking a breath because she gets winded, coughs, or her voice gets tired. If you get winded too, you may need to stop and take in a slow, deep inhale so you can continue laughing. The more you laugh, the bigger your exhalations will become, the better your oxygen exchange, and the healthier you'll be.

Stretch Out Your Laughter

Here's the next step to becoming familiar with the experience of intentional laugher. When you reach your arms above your head, lean back, stretch, and point your chin up, you'll notice your throat is wide open. Now a deeper laughter sound can emerge. This Celebration Stretch opens your lungs and expands your breathing. Your mind and body are connected, so a joyful posture, such as this one, releases chemicals in your brain even before you start to laugh.

Maybe you like power. Great! People who stand in akimbo, or Superman Pose—with feet wide apart, hands in fists resting on hips, back straight, and confidence oozing—feel more powerful. Choose either the Celebration Stretch or Superman Pose or alternate between the two poses and start your power *Ha-Ha-Has*. The more you practice deep belly breathing, Laughter Breaths, and stretching out your laughter, the longer you will be able to sustain a laugh. Next, let's explore how adding joyful play (in place of humor) evokes powerful belly laughter.

Play— The Magic Ingredient of Intentional Laughter

> "Playfulness is a gift
> that grants you great power.
> It allows you to transform
> the very things that you take
> seriously into opportunities
> for shared laughter."
>
> Bernard DeKoven, *A Playful Path*

The notion of play typically triggers an image of young children joyfully engaging in imaginative, creative games they make up as they go. According to Maria Montessori, physician and educator, play is the work of the child. Children play spontaneously, with wild abandon and wonderment.

While easy to recognize, play is difficult to define. Play has many qualities. Play is fun, engaging, and sometimes silly. Play is not only an activity we engage in voluntarily, it's a mindset, a way of being. It's not serious. Playful activities call on us to be creative, spontaneous, responsive, and uninhibited. From giggles to guffaws, and everything in between, shared laughter is one of the most recognizable sounds of play. Play brings us fully into the present. We leave our worries and concerns behind.

What happens to us as we grow up? Many adults find it difficult to let go and play. At school we focus, at work we perform, at home we recover—there's seemingly no time for play, little time for leisure. With our responsibilities piling up, we may not believe we deserve to have fun until we have accomplished all there is to do. As we grow, we're encouraged to leave the childlike parts of ourselves on the playground and not carry them into adulthood.

Insufficient play is called play deprivation, a phrase coined by Dr. Stuart Brown, physician, psychiatrist, clinical researcher, play scholar, and founder of the National Institute for Play. His message is that playing and feeling playful is seriously important for a healthy life. Adults who engage in play tend to enjoy life more than serious adults. He contends that play gives us energy, eases our burdens, and enlivens us. Brown said, "The ability to play is critical not only to being happy, but also to sustaining social relationships and being a creative, innovative person."[1]

He popularized the idea of play for adults.

Primed for Play

Play is the final element of our formula, Anatomy of a Laugh. Madan Kataria's four elements of Laughter Yoga—clapping, laughing, breathing, and playing—inspired our own formula: smile ~ breathe ~ play. For us, the simple act of smiling often leads to laughter. Another way to ease into laughter is to practice making laughter sounds with Laughter Breaths. As you focus on smiles with Smile-Ups and breathing with Laughter Breaths, laughter becomes more comfortable. You're primed for play. We've found that play leads to more contagious and sustained giggles, chuckles, and guffaws. Belly laughs erupt more easily when the imagination is engaged, or when you participate in a joyful activity within a fun and playful environment.

Permission to Play

Many adults find it difficult to let go and play. Some of us won't even consider play—it's not at all on our radar. Perhaps that's because, with our many responsibilities, we find it nearly impossible to stop and refresh ourselves. We rarely daydream

---

[1] Stuart Brown, MD, *Play: How It Shapes the Brain, Opens the Imagination, and Invigorates the Soul* (New York: Avery, 2009).

or take creative breaks. As adults, we often need reminders, permission, and encouragement to let go of our inhibitions and slow down. This enables us to find our playful selves, who may have been left behind.

Inner Child Permission Slip

Play is the magic ingredient in our formula. When Rachael was able to stop judging herself, she gave her Inner Child permission to come out and play. Once out of her own way, play naturally happened and she began to experiment more successfully with purposeful, playful laughter.

PERMISSION TO PLAY

It's your time to play.

To: My Inner Child
From: Me
Re: **Come Out and Play—Permission Granted**

This voucher allows for
one fun, fantastic, and unfettered play session.
(You may play alone or with others as your heart desires.)

Clap freely ～ Run wildly ～ Jump for joy

Look for glimmers of giggles or frolicking fields
of flowers along your way.

Fully transferable   Redeem any time   Unlimited uses

Expiration Date: Never

> **SPEED BUMP**
>
> ### Are You Play Deprived?
>
> Are you play deprived?
>
> Do you often feel irritated or stressed?
>
> Are you facing endless cycles of chores and tasks?
>
> How do you dig yourself out of play-deprived adulthood?
>
> Pair a fun activity with the dreaded one to help shift your focus.
>
> For example, dance to your favorite music while cleaning.
>
> What can you discover as you adopt the mindset of a child and consciously add play?

Applaud Your Inner Child

When you were young, how did it feel to discover something new? Or to finish something?

You'd grin from ear to ear with pride. You had nothing to hide. Nothing to prove. You were fully present, utterly joyful.

You have a precious little child inside.

And it's *you*.

Now clap your hands with excitement as you smile broadly. (You may need to put the book down.)

Clap soft. Clap hard!

Inhale deeply.

As you exhale, say, *Ha-Ha-Ha!* Let the titters trickle out.

Applaud yourself. You're a kid again; you just did something silly.

Let's Take a Trip to the Playground

Becoming playful, embodying a playful spirit, and curiously allowing yourself to be in wonderment is worthwhile. The play is not outside of us. We have an inner playground. Imagine yourself on a magnificent playground. Create a mental image with details of what you see: the other kids playing, the blue sky, a sunny day, puffy clouds. Can you see it—your clothes, the bright smile on your face, the butterflies in your stomach either from excitement or a bit of nervousness? Can you hear the sounds? Can you feel laughter bubbling, ready to burst forth?

Children love to swing because gliding effortlessly in the air in the secure seat of the swing feels like flying. As they pump their legs, or get pushed from behind, they imagine themselves soaring through the clouds like a bird way up high.

Let's try swinging with giggles. As we move back and forth, imagine pumping higher and higher. The smiles expand. Giggles become chuckles that turn into howls of laughter. You may need to sit for this one as you act out swinging.

LAUGHTER GAME

Swing Like a Child and Play

Rush to an empty swing. Wiggle into the seat as you clasp the chains.

1. Walk your feet backwards to get started.
2. Lean back, lift your feet off the ground, and extend your legs forward.

You're in the air, swinging!

3. Bend forward, still holding on to the chains, tuck your feet under the swing.
4. Lean back and extend your legs forward. Tickle the sky with your toes.
5. Tuck your feet and pump again.
6. Repeat until you're as high as you can go.

Feel the wind on your face and the thrill of soaring. Go ahead. Whoop with laughter!

Rules of the Game

The goal of a *Laughter Game* is to have fun and laugh, without keeping score. Typically, for adults, games include rules, scorekeeping, and competition—someone wins and someone loses. In *Laughter Games*, there are only winners! Everyone plays and has fun. Eye contact is strongly encouraged since laughter is contagious. Connecting with each other through eye contact helps lower inhibitions, begins to build trust, and strengthens relationships. At the start of any laughter session, we agree to support each other in laughter. The rule is: no judgment, of yourself or others, ever!

The no-judgment rule from Dr. Kataria is something we emphasize and return to during a session when any discomfort surfaces among the participants. The environment of total acceptance, without judgment, makes the space feel safe for everyone. Laughter as a game and activity is intentionally designed to be cooperative, not competitive. The cooperative spirit is an essential component of Dr. Kataria's goal to use laughter as a vehicle to bring world peace and combat bullying.

Putting It All Together

So, what about adults and play? We suggest learning from children. If we take the chance and are willing to shift our thinking to let ourselves go, we can derive pure pleasure just from being fun and playful.

During Sarah's laughter sessions, she has noticed that some groups, though they enthusiastically embrace Smile-Ups and eagerly try Laughter Breaths, become uncertain what to do when encouraged to experiment with different chortles and guffaws triggered by *Laughter Games*. With careful instructions, Sarah walks them through the steps of each game. If the laughter is slow to come, she coaches them to put their imaginations to work. "Picture yourself, right now, in your favorite place chuckling with a fun person. See yourself slapping your knees as you roll on the ground with uncontrollable, side-splitting laughter." Sarah emits a contagious chortle as she describes possible scenarios, encouraging participants to laugh along with the mental images of themselves engaged in play. "Perhaps you're with a friend on a picnic and a chipmunk comes along and takes one of your homemade cookies, then turns and looks at you as if to ask for more." Unlikely fantasies can sometimes spark the giggles. Some participants can't keep from tittering along, and soon Sarah's prompts and her own laughs help the joyous sounds flow more freely. At the end of the game, Sarah will often ask people to share what they imagined. The sharing inspires others in the group and often leads to more laughter as the scenarios are retold.

 The nature of the laughter tells Sarah what's happening in the room. The more play, the more genuine and full-bodied the laughter. Without play, Sarah suggests, laughter is simply noise. Once you add imaginative play, contagious chuckles pave the way for full participation and lead to a joyous experience. Feedback from participants confirms that igniting the imagination makes it easier to be playful and sustain the laughter.

 We often contemplate which comes first, the laughter or the play. The more we allow our imaginations to run wild, the greater the laughter. At the same time, we are aware that the more we give in to that unabashed laughter, the more our imaginations soar. Chicken - egg - laughter - play? You decide.

> **JUMP START**
>
> ### Time Yourself
>
> Let's see how long you can sustain a laugh until you have to take a breath.
>
> Set a timer for thirty seconds. Start laughing just as you push start.
>
> Take as many breaths while laughing as you need to so you can keep those full-bodied laughter exhales coming.
>
> Visualize amusing scenarios to spur on and sustain the giggles.
>
> Once you reach thirty seconds, reset the timer for sixty seconds.
>
> As you practice, you'll continue to expand the duration of your laughter as you build to a full fifteen minutes! (Breathe as needed.)

Don't Skip the Fun!

Now we're going to actually skip. Skipping is playful and directly engages our sense of fun. For us, it's hard to hear the word skip without immediately picturing friends, hand in hand, heading gleefully to somewhere, or nowhere. Let's start by skipping with your fingers because it's easy and you don't get out of breath.

| LAUGHTER GAME |

Finger Skipping

It's nearly impossible to skip with a straight face. As a catalyst for activating play, let's skip with our fingers.

1. Place one hand palm up.
2. Pretend two fingers of your other hand are little legs and feet.
3. Laugh as your finger-feet skip in a circle on your palm and feel the tickle on your hand.
4. Continue to skip your finger-feet up your arm and across your chest.
5. Switch hands and skip down the other arm, laughing along the way.

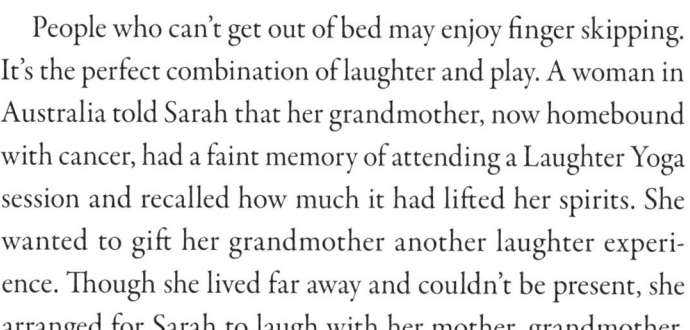

People who can't get out of bed may enjoy finger skipping. It's the perfect combination of laughter and play. A woman in Australia told Sarah that her grandmother, now homebound with cancer, had a faint memory of attending a Laughter Yoga session and recalled how much it had lifted her spirits. She wanted to gift her grandmother another laughter experience. Though she lived far away and couldn't be present, she arranged for Sarah to laugh with her mother, grandmother, and caregiver. Afterward, she called Sarah with gratitude. Her family was able to create precious memories with shared games and giggles rather than focus on the illness and its limitations. Feet-skipping was not an option for her grandmother, but the finger-skipping led to cheerful chuckles.

Office hallways and city sidewalks are perfect for skipping with your feet. Next time you're in the office, don't *skip* lunch—skip *to* lunch. Feel grateful. Skip for joy, YIPPEE! Get playful. Inside, outside, in a straight line, or in a circle. Imagine you're a kid and let yourself giggle. Grab a friend or colleague and keep skipping while you laugh in tandem.

Why skip? Not only does skipping almost always trigger laughs and giggles, it burns twice as many calories as walking. It's easy on your joints, sparks happiness and joy, restores childlike wonder, and helps you feel energized and fully present.

Smiling helps us open the door as we practice laughing on purpose, and breathing carries us through the physical act of laughing. Clapping and skipping help bring our energy up and usher us into the play state where we are surrounded by joyful laughter.

Now you know our formula for purposeful, playful laughter. You've practiced smiling and learned the value of deep breathing and powerfully exhaling with *Ha-Ha-Has*. You're armed with a special permission slip to remind you to let your Inner Child out to play. We want to be sure you have a full spectrum of good reasons to engage in giggles, chuckles, and belly laughs. Read the next chapter to learn some of the delightful discoveries we made while researching all kinds of laughter. You'll find a lot of motivation to practice laughing out loud and to develop a powerful life-long laughter habit.

"Of all the gifts bestowed by nature on human beings, hearty laughter must be close to the top."

Norman Cousins, Author

Four

Laughter Is More than Child's Play

The magic of our laughter formula is that once you start to experiment with smiling, breathing, and playing, there are some immediate rewards. The advantages of regular deep belly laughter extend across the physical, emotional, and mental arenas, and are specifically useful for stress relief, pain relief, and heart health. Laughing is good for you! It's one of the most accessible and enjoyable things you can do to take care of yourself. The ability to laugh is in your DNA. It's designed to protect and nurture you. It's free, and you don't need a prescription.

In this chapter we will describe some of the most significant discoveries we unearthed in our research. We'll look at science. We'll also share what others have shared with us—how empowering it is for people when they learn the information we share, apply it, and directly experience the benefits for themselves. As you can imagine, we get excited when we receive positive feedback about our work. The on-the-spot impact is often remarkable to us, even though we've come to expect these success stories, having had similar experiences ourselves. You can train yourself to think of playful laughter as a useful tool. Refer often to the persuasive information in this chapter. The myriad benefits of deep belly laughs will ensure you're motivated to jiggle your belly on a regular basis.

The Brilliant Physiology of Laughter

A key discovery for Rachael was the book, *Laughter and Health*, written in 1928 by Dr. James Joseph Walsh, who was a physician, PhD professor of medicine, medical director, and author. Walsh notes that humorous laughter has been recognized as good medicine for centuries. He asserts laughter is a key component of preventive medicine since hearty laughter causes the diaphragm to vibrate which in turn stimulates all of the organs of the body, enhancing their optimal functioning. He speaks about the value of creating a life-long laughter habit and highlights the vital role laughter plays as we age. He includes chapters on each organ of the body and details laughter's impact on the mind and laughter's role in surgery, both preoperatively and as the patient convalesces.

Walsh shines a light on two groups of people: those who laugh only when they have to and those who laugh whenever they can. He concludes that those who laugh often enjoy higher functioning bodily organs, have more physical energy, and derive greater enjoyment from life. Dr. Walsh created a mathematical expression for a person's health: health varies in direct proportion to how much a person laughs: —H. ∝ L.[2]

Walsh brilliantly explains the impact of a two-to-three-minute belly laugh not only on the lungs, but on the entire body. "In the course of a single minute every cell of tissue in the body, including the brain cells, will have been exposed to an increased amount of oxygen as a consequence of a hearty laugh."[3]

It seems the more you laugh, the healthier you'll be.

You Stress, I Stress, We All Stress

Stress is part of life. Good stress is called *eustress*, the feeling you get when you are excited. *Eustress* causes your pulse to accelerate and your hormones to increase. This kind of stress is short-term and can be useful when it compels you to perform at a high level, as in a life-threatening situation like escaping from a burning building, or when accomplishing a goal like taking a difficult exam or finishing a marathon. Bad stress, on the other hand, wears you out and can be harmful to your health. Chronic stress suppresses the immune system, ultimately resulting in illness, as illustrated in Rachael's story when she was hospitalized at age sixteen.

Silent and invisible, stress drowns rational thinking, kindles negative emotions, and fuels self-sabotaging conduct. Just because we aren't experiencing the outward signs of

---

2 James Walsh, *Laughter and Health* (New York: D. Appleton and Company, 1928), xi.

3 Walsh, *Laughter and Health,* 29.

stress overload (yet) doesn't mean chronic stress isn't doing a number on us internally. According to the Mayo Clinic's healthy lifestyle information on stress management, several health problems, including high blood pressure, heart disease, stroke, obesity, and diabetes, may result from chronic stress.

FUN FACT

Stimulating the Vagus Nerve with Laughter

When we learned about the amazing vagus nerve, Walsh's observations about the effect of deep belly laughing on the key body systems came to mind. As the longest cranial nerve in the body (see illustration), it is the essential component of the body's parasympathetic nervous system responsible for *rest and digest* as opposed to *fight or flight*. Increased vagus nerve activity directly impacts the mood, the mindset, and even the voice. It regulates internal organ functions such as digestion, heart rate, and respiratory rate, as well as vasomotor activity, and certain reflex actions, such as coughing, sneezing, swallowing, and vomiting. All five lobes of the lungs are utilized in belly breathing which effectively stimulates the vagus nerve and activates the relaxation response. Laughter consistently appears on lists of natural ways to stimulate the vagus nerve.

Have you heard of a meta-analysis? Simply put, it is a compilation of scientific research, a study of studies, that summarizes the most up-to-date understanding on a given topic. A 2023 meta-analysis of laughter's impact on the stress response showed cortisol, the stress hormone, decreased after spontaneous laughter when compared to other activities. The evaluation of eight studies concluded that laughter could be used "as a potential adjunctive medical therapy to improve well-being."[4]

These studies also found laughter that's associated with optimism, positively impacted cardiovascular health and exceptional longevity. They also linked laughter to increased pain tolerance as well as enhanced well-being in rehabilitation, psychiatry, and oncology.

Laughter helps us cope with and bounce back from daily tensions as it defuses and limits the negative impacts of stress, like looming deadlines and toddler tantrums, as well as life-altering ones, like death and divorce. When you drop a glass dish, and it breaks, or your car won't start . . . push pause by taking a deep breath to stop stress in its tracks. Exhale as you let go with a few vigorous *Ha-Ha-Has!* Begin to recognize upsets, big and small, as opportunities for intentional smiles and laughter.

---

4   C.K. Kramer and C. B. Leitao, (2023) "Laughter as medicine: A systematic review and meta-analysis of interventional studies evaluating the impact of spontaneous laughter on cortisol levels." *PLoS ONE* 18, no. 5 (May 23, 2023): e0286260. https://journals.plos.org/plosone/article?id=10.1371/journal.pone.0286260.

LAUGHTER BREAK

 Crumple Your Stress

It's time to take all the stress you're feeling and crumple it up like a piece of paper and toss it back and forth from one hand to the other.

Laugh out loud as you toss it into the air and watch it evaporate.

Got lots of stress? Feel free to fill a trash can with your stress balls.

Chemical Effects of Laughter on the Body

We can all benefit from a daily DOSE of Laughter. How we're doing physically, mentally, and emotionally affects the production and distribution of both happy and stress hormones, which always work in tandem. Depression and stress are often lumped together in conversations about mood. Stress causes the body to produce cortisol, most commonly known as the stress hormone. Laughter reduces chronic stress by flooding the body with powerful feel-good chemicals. These chemicals can easily be remembered with the acronym DOSE: Dopamine, Oxytocin, Serotonin, and Endorphins. Blocking the production of cortisol lets the body know stress is no longer necessary. As stress decreases, depression can also ease, paving the way toward joy.

Teaching people about the body's chemical response to smiling and laughter empowers them to diffuse stressful moments and upsets, without much time or effort. One of Sarah's clients shared her experience after she and her nine-year-old son attended a laughter session together. During a minor argument at dinner, her son left the table in a huff. A few minutes later, she found him in front of the mirror using one of the laughter tools they had just learned to calm down and cheer up. How exciting—her son was so empowered at such a young age! You can limit the negative impacts of stress at any age and use laughter as an easily accessible tool for self-care.

We were fascinated to discover the book, *Deep Survival: Who Lives, Who Dies, and Why*, by Laurence Gonzales. The combination of adventure, survival science, and practical advice inspired us, especially Rachael, to get more comfortable laughing out loud. We were delighted to read that the common denominator among people who survive serious accidents, adventure mishaps, and catastrophic events is their ability to laugh at their situation and create a playful mindset. Reading this, Rachael was eager to experiment. She found that playful laughter not only helped her control stress but could help her to prepare for future emergencies.

Laughter sends "chemical signals to actively inhibit the firing of nerves in the amygdala, thereby dampening fear . . . [which helps] temper negative emotions."[5]

Survivors, especially those who manage to persevere through horrible situations, use play to put themselves in touch with their environment, and use laughter to help manage their feelings of being threatened. The prefrontal cortex is stimulated during laughter which motivates us, helps us feel good, and alleviates frustration and anxiety.[6]

Norman Cousins— "Ambassador from the Land of Yes"

Norman Cousins and his book, *Anatomy of an Illness as Perceived by the Patient*, is central to almost all research discussed today about the health benefits of laughter. Cousins was a renowned journalist and editor of *Saturday Review* magazine.

---

5   Laurence Gonzales, *Deep Survival: Who Lives, Who Dies, and Why* (New York: W. W. Norton & Company, 2005), 41.

6   Gonazles, *Deep Survival,* 41.

In 1964, he was hospitalized with excruciating pain and near-paralysis of his back, neck, legs, and jaw. The diagnosis: *ankylosing spondylitis,* a rare autoimmune disorder that causes severe inflammation of joints and ligaments, particularly of the spine. He was given just six months to live and told to put his affairs in order. Conventional medicine offered Cousins little relief, and his debilitation and suffering continued.

It was then Cousins decided to fight for his life. He recalled Hans Selye's book, *The Stress of Life,* from which he learned that negative emotions such as fear, suppressed rage, and frustration are linked to adrenal exhaustion. Cousins theorized the opposite must also be true. He believed the positive emotions of love, hope, and faith, combined with laughter and a fierce will to live, would bring about the healing he sought.

Working closely with his physician, Cousins began a regimen of high doses of vitamin C and hearty laughter while watching old *Candid Camera* episodes and *Marx Brothers* movies. Cousins made the *joyous discovery* that just ten minutes of belly laughing gave him at least two hours of pain-free sleep.[7]

Despite his doctor's original grim prognosis, Cousins went on to live another 25 years.

Inspired by Cousins' story, we were delighted to find his youngest daughter, Sarah Shapiro, who agreed to speak with us. She summarized her father's overriding message. It was not that laughter alone can cure illness, but that "Laughter is a metaphor for all the positive emotions—for love, hope, and faith."[8]

---

[7] Norman Cousins, *Anatomy of an Illness as Perceived by the Patient: Reflections on Healing and Regeneration* (New York, London: W.W. Norton, 1979), 43.

[8] Sarah Shapiro (author) in discusson with the authors, October 22, 2020.

She described her father as "an emissary from the Bright Side . . . an ambassador from the land of Yes." She explained, "He had been honing the art of positive thinking ever since his first decade when . . . he consciously cultivated optimism."[9]

Cousins exemplified the potential of laughter to distract us from pain and minimize its effects. Upon his return to good health, he sought out Dr. Lee Berk, the world's current authority on mirthful laughter and humor, at Loma Linda University in California. Cousins sought funding for scientific research to prove what he had directly experienced.

Lifestyle Impacts Health

Dr. Berk was inspired by the idea in Proverbs 17:22, that a merry heart is like good medicine, but sadness can lead to disease. He proposed that this verse in Proverbs refers to the medical science of psychoneuroimmunology and integrative medicine. In a 2015 interview, Berk discussed the positive health outcomes for those who engaged in joyful laughter, validating what we learned from Dr. Walsh and offering further evidence of the power of laughter as experienced by Norman Cousins.[10]

It was Dr. Berk who demonstrated that laughter and exercise have similar effects on the body. He coined the term

---

9 Sarah Shapiro, *An Audience of One and Other Stories* (New York: Mosaica Press, Inc., 2021), 247.

10 Alita Byrd, "World Authority on Laughter Talks Us Through the Research," *Spectrum* magazine, August 9, 2015. https://spectrummagazine.org/news/world-authority-laughter-talks-us-through-research/.

laughercise. Over the course of his career, he substantiated the ties between the physical, emotional, and stress-related benefits of laughter. His research includes studies on the impact of laughter on the nervous and immune systems, revealing that laughter reduces the production of stress hormones.[11]

Berk was a true advocate of preventative medicine. He believed it was important to recognize that medication is not the only way to optimize health. As a preventive care specialist, Berk suggests that mirthful laughter is a key player in overall wellness, joining a balanced diet, good sleep, and moderate exercise to help combat stress and build immunity.

While studying the neuroendocrine and immune effects of positive emotions and laughter, Berk found that merely anticipating a positive laughter experience can have the same effect as actually laughing.[12]

Just as your mouth salivates when you anticipate and think about a delicious dinner, your immune system responds positively when you anticipate laughter. Dr. Lee Berk proved it.

---

11 Lee S Berk, MPH, DrPH, David L. Felten, MD PhD, Stanley A. Tan, MD, PhD, Barry B. Bittman, MD, and James Westengard, BS, "Modulation of Neuroimmune Parameters During the Eustress of Humor-Associated Mirthful Laughter," *Alternative Therapies in Health and Medicine,* March 2001;7(2):(62-76).

12 American Physiological Society, "Anticipating A Laugh Reduces Our Stress Hormones, Study Shows," *ScienceDaily.* https://www.sciencedaily.com/releases/2008/04/080407114617.htm#.

> **SPEED BUMP**
>
> ## Remembering Joyful Moments
>
> Imagine sharing a smile. Do you feel more connected even though the other person isn't in front of you right now? Feel the energy generated by the memory of the shared smile.
>
> Think about a a time you laughed with glee. You've just formed a picture of a joyful you!
>
> Summon another cheerful moment as you smile, then giggle.
>
> How was your experience of smiling and laughing impacted by the feelings of joy you recalled?
>
> Next time you're feeling down, reflect on how simply thinking about joyous moments creates a smile or a laugh, which can elevate your mood.

We want to give you all the tools you need to strengthen your laughter muscles and to achieve sustained laughter by taking charge of how long you laugh. Belly laughs are a critical component of sustained laughter. It's time to try a belly laugh for yourself. Belly laughs involve the jiggling of the belly. When we laugh vigorously, the exhale during the laughter causes the diaphragm to massage the internal organs. We sometimes refer to belly laughter as robust, full-bodied, sustained, or hearty laughter. No matter what you call it, deep belly laughter is the goal.

> **JUMP START**
>
> ### Jiggling Belly Laughs
>
> Inhale deeply.
>
> Now, as you exhale, squeeze out a boisterous string of *Ha-Ha-Has,* building to as big a laugh as you can.
>
> Do it again while consciously jiggling your belly until natural gales of laughter take over.
>
> Feel free to use your hands to help you jiggle your belly.
>
> ---
>
> Just taking the action of jiggling will help jump-start deeper laughter. No self-judgment allowed. This is your first attempt. You'll get better at it.

Laughter for Your Heart

When Sarah met cardiologist Dr. Michael Miller at a Laughter Conference in 2015, his book, *Heal your Heart: The Positive Emotions Prescription to Prevent and Reverse Heart Disease*, had just been published. Sarah wondered if she had wandered into a medical lecture. Dr. Miller was explaining his research about how mental stress can constrict the endothelium (inner lining) of blood vessels, which can lead to high blood pressure, coronary artery disease, heart attack, or stroke. When Miller started talking about his study that revealed people with heart disease were forty percent less likely to laugh than people of the same age without disease, her ears perked up. She knew she was in the right place. Miller explained further studies indicated that the endothelium relaxed and expanded with laughter, increasing blood flow. He said, "The magnitude of change we saw in the endothelium after laughing was consistent and similar to the benefit we might see with aerobic exercise or statin use."[13]

That absolutely clinched it. For years, Sarah had been offering free weekly laughter calls to anyone interested. Armed with Dr. Miller's research, she was sure she'd be able to encourage more people to share in regular, hearty laughter.

Chapter 3 of Miller's book begins with Miller describing how he somberly informs his heart patients "there's one thing they absolutely must do in order to make a successful recovery after a cardiac event . . . go home and laugh until they cry."[14]

For anyone concerned about their heart health, we have plenty of laughter tools to help you follow doctor's orders.

---

13   Press Release from the European Society of Cardiology. "Laughter has a positive impact on vascular function," (August 28, 2011). https://www.escardio.org/The-ESC/Press-Office/Press-releases/Laughter-has-a-positive-impact-on-vascular-function.

14   Michael Miller, MD, *Heal Your Heart: The Positive Emotions Prescription to Prevent and Reverse Heart Disease* (Rodale Press, 2014), page 65.

FUN FACT

Laughter By-Product, Nitric Oxide, Wins Awards

Nitric oxide, not to be confused with the anesthetic drug, nitrous oxide, (laughing gas), was named 1992 Molecule of the Year. In his book, Dr. Miller explains nitric oxide causes vasodilation of the blood vessels and reduces inflammation, cholesterol plaque, and clot formation—the same benefits we get from laughing.[15]

In 1998, nitric oxide once again took center stage as three United States pharmacologists: Robert F. Furchgott, PhD, Louis J. Ignarro, PhD, and Ferid Murad, MD, PhD, were awarded joint Nobel Prizes for Physiology and Medicine for discovering that nitric oxide is a signaling molecule in the cardiovascular system. It relaxes smooth muscle cells, causing blood vessels to dilate, increasing blood flow, and decreasing blood pressure.[16]

---

15 Miller, *Heal Your Heart,* pages 71-74.

16 Press Release, October 12, 1998 *The Nobel Prize.* "The Nobel Prize In Physiology or Medicine 1998" *The Nobel Prize,* nobelprize.org/medicine.

LAUGHTER BREAK

Make Your Own Nitric Oxide

Ready to produce some nitric oxide to benefit your heart right now?

Let's do another deep belly laugh.

Inhale deeply.

Jiggle your belly on the exhale as you let go with another boisterous round of *Ha-Ha-Ha*s. Remember it's okay to use your hands to jiggle that belly!

Physical benefits of robust laughter, whether caused by humor, self-generated, or laughing with others in a group, offer persuasive reasons to deepen your relationship with laughter. The combination of focusing more attention on smiling, breathing, playing, and laughing causes ripple effects in many areas of life. Now that we have a deeper understanding of the science of laughter, let's put it into practice. With everyday life as our laboratory, let's play . . . with all these laughter types and sounds:

"To truly laugh, you must be able to take your pain, and play with it!"

Charlie Chaplin, Actor

Five

Laughter Games

Why play games? Because they're fun! *Laughter Games* supercharge the laughter experience. Many of the games we've included come from Dr. Kataria's foundational exercises. We prefer the term *Laughter Games* because we want to emphasize the importance of play in the process. *Laughter Games* engage our imaginations, liberate our insecurities, and deliver the health benefits of deep hearty laughter. Games help us generate and sustain the belly laughs. As you play a series of games with small clapping transitions or deep breathing in between, you will be more able to continue laughing than if you were just listening to jokes. We use *Laughter Games* to create a playful exploration of any situation.

What is a *Laughter Game*? A *Laughter Game* is a short activity designed to trigger gentle giggles, elicit contagious chuckles, and ultimately stimulate full-bodied belly laughs releasing tears of joy. When you blend smiling, breathing, and play with laughter, you're winning the *Laughter Game* no matter how hard or how long you laugh.

Being playful can help you adopt the mindset of an eager, curious child—a perfect template for overcoming stress and becoming more light-hearted. We invite you to take a risk and ease out of your comfort zone. At your own pace, step into the space of childlike play. Remember to bring your imagination.

There are three types of *Laughter Games*: those we play alone, those we play with a friend, and those we play in a group. As you read the book, play the games. Use a mirror for added fun, or invite a friend or group of friends to join you. The more people involved in the play, the further the laughter will spread.

Sarah told Rachael that Madan Kataria wakes up every morning and laughs *alone* for forty minutes. Rachael decided to try to wake up and laugh for *one* minute before getting out of bed. Overtaken by concerns that her husband would notice her laughing alone, she hesitated. Even if he just chuckled, her personal inhibitions, embarrassment, and self-judgment prevented her from laughing out loud. Here's the spark of creativity Sarah suggested to help Rachael overcome her discomfort.

Welcome to Our Laughter Family!

Share your contact info to receive

FREE! FREE! FREE!
- Laughter event invites
- Exciting insider perks
- Advanced notice of new offerings

Join us here

DiscoverThePowerOfLaughter.com
We promise not to share your info or fill your inbox with emails.

LAUGHTER GAME

Joyful Giggles

Start your day feeling joyful and grateful before you get out of bed. Wake up your imagination and let it be your guide as you play out this scene:

1. Imaginary smiley faces emerge from your pillow.
2. Smile back! With fun as your guide, begin to giggle.
3. Your giggles activate the smiley faces, turning them into bouncing laughter emojis.
4. Wiggle your toes as laughter spreads throughout your body.
5. Feel the energy.
6. Picture the giggles getting louder and bouncing on your belly, catapulting you out of bed.

Sharing a bed? Deepen your relationship with your partner or pet by making eye contact, doing Smile-Ups, and giggling together. Laughter is a huge gift. Laugh with gratitude and increased vitality. Give yourself permission to be playful.

SPEED BUMP

Perhaps You're Thinking…

I don't feel ready to laugh yet. I had trouble picturing laughing giggles on my pillow. It feels ridiculous to generate laughter like this.

You may want to find a video of babies laughing, or animal videos, anything likely to bring a smile to your face. You may also use memories of yourself laughing to help you smile.

Notice what kinds of images trigger smiles and which ones elicit a giggle or chuckle.

Now try again to picture those smiles on your pillow.

Take note of where you are on the *Laughter Participation Scale* at this moment.

By looking at the scale, and recalling the benefits from the previous chapter, can you coax yourself into curiosity?

Invite Your Inner Child Out to Play

Start with a smile, a clap, a chuckle, whatever feels good. If you feel uncomfortable or embarrassed, take a deep breath, renew your resolve, and remember no judgment allowed. You've got this! The goal is to sustain full-bodied laughter for fifteen to thirty seconds, or laugh until you cry in every game to get the highest heart rate and the best workout. Practice leads to mastery.

LAUGHTER PARTICIPATION SCALE

 Uninhibited and Free

 Eager

 Engaged

 Willing to Experiment

 Curious

 Cautious

 Skeptical

 Fearful

 Not Interested at All

Warm Up with Smile-Ups

Do you remember the Smile-Up sequence—Smile. Relax. Smile. Relax. Repeat ten times? Smile-Ups really help you loosen up. As you intentionally work through ten Smile-Ups, try this variation: Let your smiles release gentle chuckles!

LAUGHTER GAME

Unzip Your Smile

Pantomime zipping and unzipping your smile.

1. Use your hand to unzip your smile as you move from one side of your mouth toward the other.
2. Move your hand in the opposite direction to zip it closed.
3. As you move through ten repetitions, use different types of zippers:

Unzip from the middle of your mouth, widening your smile from ear to ear.

Play with a circular zipper as your smiles expand into laughter.

Switch things up for extra fun as you zip and unzip in a diagonal direction.

As you feel your face stretching, massage your cheek muscles and encourage yourself to generate a healthy dose of fun, play, and intention.

Energize with Clapping

Give yourself a round of applause! Why? Clapping stimulates the twenty-plus pressure points on the palms and fingers, which correspond to nearly all the organs in your body. You may be able to clap your way to health like seventy-six-year-old, K.C. Bhardwaj, a man in India who says he cured his glaucoma by clapping for thirty minutes every morning for a year.[17] Clapping can also energize you before a meeting, after a big lunch, or while prepping for an exercise workout. It can also be a way to appreciate yourself, just for showing up in any given moment.

We clap during laughter sessions for many reasons. Clapping expresses enthusiasm and delight, in addition to celebration, approval, and affirmation. During a laughter session, we transition between games by using a round of clapping. We're bringing our hands together to motivate ourselves with applause, to keep our energy flowing, to move with rhythm, and to boost collaboration.

Here are three clapping-chanting games to help you get the hang of it. You may recognize the first two as typical Laughter Yoga transitions.

---

[17] Sebastian Gendry, "Clapping Hands Can Change Your Life: Science, Testimonial, Video," *Laughter Online University.* https://www.laughteronlineuniversity.com/clapping-hands/#google_vignette.

LAUGHTER GAME

Ho-Ho! Ha-Ha-Ha!

1. Bend your elbows with your hands at chest/eye level as you get ready to laugh.
2. Spread your fingers wide.
3. Clap two times as you chant, *Ho-Ho! (Pause)*
4. Clap three times as you chant, *Ha-Ha-Ha!*
5. Do the entire five-clap sequence three times for a total of fifteen claps. Get faster as you go along.

LAUGHTER GAME

Very Good, Very Good... YAY!

1. Clap two times and then raise your hands in the air.
2. With each clap, say, *Very Good!*
3. Shout, *YAY!* As you raise your hands in the air.
4. Repeat three times - Clap, Clap, Raise - as you say, *Very Good, Very Good, Yay!*

Don't be afraid to clap and laugh like a kid. After Rachael took the Laughter Yoga leader training, she played it safe and started by teaching some of the really easy games to her two-year-old granddaughter, Temima. Most two-year-olds can clap and won't be concerned with getting it right or looking good. Temima joyfully followed the directions, changing it slightly. Instead of saying, *Very Good, Very Good, Yay!* as had been demonstrated, she said, *Very Good, Very Good, Yippee!* followed by some joyful laughs from her grandmother. Success is sweet.

LAUGHTER GAME

Very Good, Very Good, YAY!—Choose Your Favorite Language

Let's travel the world. Pack your laughter accents as we play the game in different languages.

1. Let's practice the words for *Very* and *Good* in Italian, *Molto* and *Bene*.
2. Clap each time you say, *Molto Bene*, as you did when you said, *Very Good*.
3. In place of raising both hands and shouting, YAY!, use both index fingers to touch your belly and push in as you shout, *Si!*
4. Your smile widens as you say, *Si!* Hold your grin for a second before clapping again.
5. Repeat the whole phrase, *Molte Bene, Molte Bene, Si!* three times.
6. Practice and play to master your accent.

Now you're practically fluent in Italian!

Here are a few languages to play with—feel free to add your own.

- "Muy Bien, Muy Bien…Si!" (Spanish)
- "Tove Me'od Tove Me'od…Ken!" (Hebrew)
- "Optimus Optimum…Immo Vero!" (Latin)
- "Nzuri Sana, Nzuri Sana…Ndio!" (Swahili)
- "Nagyon Jo, Nagyon Jo…Yea!" (Hungarian)

Can you feel your hands, arms, and body starting to tingle with energy? Your body is whispering, *Thank you for paying attention to me and doing fun new things.*

Typically, we stretch and breathe deeply after a few games, but you'll find your own natural rhythm. When you feel winded, stop and breathe. You may choose to breathe deeply at the end of a *Laughter Game,* before, after, or instead of a clapping transition.

Let the *Laughter Games* Begin!

We combed through our files of hundreds of *Laughter Games* and chose some of our favorites to share here. Many more are already giggling and waiting for you throughout this book as well as on our website. Exercise your creativity and adapt each game to suit you and your circumstances.

You can play *Laughter Games* anywhere. We like to get a fresh dose of positivity every day. The shower is a convenient place to start. As you grab the soap keep in mind the Yiddish proverb, "What soap is to the body, laughter is to the soul."

Sarah designed colorful plastic bottles with the words, *silly soap*, *happy hair gel*, *lather with laughter*, and *get the giggles*. She adorned her bathroom with the labeled bottles and a set of *ticklish towels* to remind her and her guests that laughter helps you freshen up.

LAUGHTER GAME

Shower Yourself with Laughter

In the shower, instead of turning on cold and hot water, turn on *giggles* and *belly laughs*.

1. Step into the shower and adjust the knobs. To the right, ramp up to *chuckles*. To the left, add *snorts* and *chortles*. Experiment to find the right mix.
2. Wiggle your fingers as the laughter cascades downward and the merriment washes over you.
3. Have fun washing with *silly soap* and *happy hair gel*.
4. Let your imagination soar as you *lather with laughter*.
5. As you rinse off, shake out the sillies and notice your positive attitude.
6. Dry off with a *ticklish towel*, which triggers new peals of laughter.

Touch is vital to our existence. Many people live alone and don't get enough hugs which is why Sarah created this game. Embracing and nurturing yourself is vital for self-love. For many of us self-love is challenging. Use this game to practice loving and hugging yourself for the gifts you offer the world.

LAUGHTER GAME

I Love Myself Laugh

1. Imagine a laughing emoji on each of your upturned palms.
2. Giggle at them as they begin to bounce with delight, multiplying as they bump into each other.
3. Spread out your arms, flinging the emojis into the air. Giggles scatter.
4. With your arms outstretched, imagine—and physically act out—gathering love from the universe and then give yourself a big laughter hug.
5. Repeat *at least* five times. You deserve it.

Sarah had the idea that if we genuinely played the I Love Myself Laugh game, there would be giggles floating around everywhere, and if someone were paying attention, they would be able to catch them.

She thought, *What a great way to extend the laughter beyond the game.* Go on an imaginary walk. Imagine something tickles your nose, your elbow, or your knee. Someone else's giggles have just landed on you—much more fun than bird droppings!

LAUGHTER GAME

Catch the Giggles

1. Notice giggles falling from the sky like raindrops.

   > Giggles on the pavement.
   > Giggles on your head.
   > Giggles sliding down your face.

2. Feel where each giggle tickles you. Touch each spot to identify where the giggle landed.

What on earth do splattering giggles feel like? It's up to you.

3. Laugh in a variety of ways.
4. When you laugh, imagine how many people are impacted by your laughter as they catch *your* giggles.

A giggle falls from the sky and goes . . .

> *SPLAT!!!*

Yes, it's raining giggles.

> *SPLAT! SPLAT! SPLAT!*

As each new giggle lands, notice the medley of joyous sounds and laugh along loudly.

Somebody, somewhere, scattered giggles, and you caught a bunch.

What a gift. Be sure to laugh as you give in to fun. Once you've caught someone's giggles, playfully share them with others. As you walk through your day, search for the giggles and savor the splattering sounds.

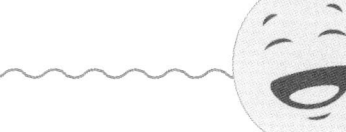

Do you remember a time when you started to laugh but it was the wrong time and wrong place for laughter—a serious conversation, a business meeting, or a funeral? You couldn't keep from laughing so you did your best to stuff it back in until you couldn't contain it any longer. The chortles and pent-up sounds came tumbling out, giving your laughter muscles a robust workout and likely causing a few raised eyebrows until you managed to gain control of yourself.

Let's try it now—use your memory to trigger the laughter.

LAUGHTER GAME

Silent Laughter

1. Begin to giggle silently, but keep your mouth closed to contain the sound.
2. As your laughter grows, cover your mouth, aware that some of the chortles are finding their voice despite your best efforts.
3. Continue to slap your knees, roll your shoulders, or crunch your body, trying to keep the guffaws from spreading.
4. When the laughter is leaking out of every pore and you can't contain it any longer, let out all your pent-up laughter in belly laughs, and laugh out loud with glee!

Does your laughter have a color? You are likely familiar with using color to reflect your mood. You may choose to wear a bright-colored shirt when feeling especially chipper or to paint a room blue to create a calming effect. Even if you've never studied the psychology of color or seen a chart pairing colors with specific emotions, this *Laughter Game* is designed to ignite your imagination and have you laughing in a full array of laughter-hued sounds and colors. This is a perfect game to play solo, with a friend, or in a group.

LAUGHTER GAME

Laugh in Color

1. Choose a paintbrush—any size will do.
2. Pantomime splattering rainbow giggles and laughter drops in the air, or on a canvas.
3. Adjust your laughter sounds to match your color palette and brush strokes.
4. Try an abstract action painting, subdued still-life, or adopt the style of your favorite artist.
5. Fill your canvas with exuberant brush strokes as you chortle and snicker in a variety of colorful hues.
6. Pour laughter on the walls, the floor, your clothes, or your friend.

Notice how the laughs vary with your choice of colors, tools, and styles.

In this chapter we've given you warm-ups and *Laughter Games* to get you started. To cool down, Laughter Yoga sessions typically end with a Laughter Meditation—several minutes of sustained laughter followed by deep breathing and relaxation. You can finish a laughter session this way whether you're with a group or laughing solo.

LAUGHTER GAME

Laughter Meditation

1. Set a timer for between one and ten minutes so you can focus on laughing, not time.
2. Find a comfortable position—sitting, standing, or even lying down.
3. Dim the lights and/or close your eyes and begin to laugh.
4. Let the laughter change. *Grin, chuckle, chortle, and guffaw.* Tune into the laughter sounds you hear.
5. As you feel the laughter subside or the timer ends, breathe—slow, deep, and steady.
6. Refreshed and energized, check in with each part of your body, and when you're ready, open your eyes.

It's Time to Assess

Once you've laughed using these games, you may feel like you've been massaged from the inside out. Having engaged in a laughter workout, do you notice greater ease in your body, increased energy, or an elevated mood? Without going to the gym, you may feel invigorated with rising confidence. We're just beginning. In the next chapter we'll discuss how to create your own *Laughter Games*. Get ready to stretch your imagination.

"At the height of laughter, the universe is flung into a kaleidoscope of new possibilities."

Jean Houston, Author

Six

Create Your Own *Laughter Games*

Cultivating creativity is a worthwhile endeavor. Generating new ways to look at life's circumstances with lenses of play and laughter is a valuable practice. To get comfortable stretching your ingenuity, simply add your own twist to any existing *Laughter Game*. Start practicing seeing things in new ways. In this chapter we'll show you how we cultivate creativity to generate new ideas for *Laughter Games*. When you find yourself in a stressful moment or needing a laugh, try one of the following techniques to unleash your creativity and make up some of your own new games.

Choose an Ordinary Object

Let's start with an ordinary object—a pencil. Pantomime using the pencil in the expected way, to write things: a love letter, a shopping list, a traffic ticket, a poem, or use it to sign an important document.

Infuse Your Chosen Object with Magical Laughing Qualities

Pretend the pencil magically giggles as you write and won't stop laughing until you join in the fun or until you put the pencil down. You could write a best-selling novel or a screen play. Laugh along as you write your dreams in your journal and watch them come true. As a traffic cop, chuckle as you notice the pencil changes the fine on the traffic ticket to $0, no matter how many times you attempt to correct it. Keep imagining the pencil's laughing antics. The magical qualities won't run out until your pencil needs sharpening.

Transform the Chosen Object into Something New

Chuckle to yourself as the pencil becomes something else in your hands. Instead of a writing utensil, pretend to wave a conductor's baton at a world-class orchestra as you laugh along with your favorite imagined music. Lick your lips in anticipation as your pencil becomes a wooden spoon you can use to mix thick, gooey cookie dough. Giggle as you realize no one can tell you not to eat the dough before it bakes. Stir a martini with a swizzle stick or cast a spell with a magic wand to de-stress your co-workers in the office.

Switch Up the Settings or Insert Characters to Trigger Additional *Laughter Games*

Let your pencil be the center of a new story or scene. Revisit the transformed object and add characters and place them in different locations or seasons. Give them different accents. Use all five senses so you can fully become the characters and situations you are conjuring. For example, become the famous conductor, Leonard Bernstein, leading a mediocre sixth grade woodwind ensemble. Instead of getting a headache from all the wrong notes, the baton (which started as a pencil) jumps from musician to musician, tickling the students, who begin to laugh in perfect harmony, and receive a standing ovation from an audience that laughs along in syncopated rhythm. See what delicious dessert you can conjure with the wooden spoon or what mysterious character consumes magical laughing martinis.

Experiment

You choose what to create and when to laugh. Try playing with different objects: a ball, a book, a key. Infuse each object with its own giggling sounds and motions. Transform the object and design a scene around it. If one object or scene falls flat, keep going until you can conjure a way to laugh. Even if you feel silly you can't get it wrong as long as you're laughing.

Add Movement and Play

When you feel stuck, loosen your body with movement and let go as you reach for childlike playfulness. You can take a break. Step outside, move to the left or right, or twirl in a circle and look anew. Notice nuances you didn't see before. Studies show spending time in nature enlivens us and enhances creativity.[18]

During Rachael's Laughter Yoga leader training, we went outside to get some fresh air. Neighborhood backyard chickens unknowingly provided inspiration for chicken dances and clucking sounds when we returned. All our inhibitions melted away after those few minutes outside.

You try it. Moving around has also been linked to increased performance on creative tests.[19] We keep the joy of movement in mind as we act out many of the scenarios we create. Add silliness. A playmate may be helpful to activate increased activity and fun.

---

18 Jill Suttie, "How Nature Can Make You Kinder, Happier, and More Creative," *Greater Good Magazine,* March 2, 2016. https://greatergood.berkeley.edu/article/item/how_nature_makes_you_kinder_happier_more_creative.

19 Bas Korsten, "Train Your Brain to Be More Creative," *Harvard Business Review,* weekly newsletter, *Ascend,* June 17, 2021. https://hbr.org/2021/06/train-your-brain-to-be-more-creative.

Samples of Successful Laughter Triggers That We Love

Here are three different examples of using shoes in playful ways to trigger laughter. Transform a shoe into a new object, infuse shoes with magical qualities, or imagine a shoe shopping experience filled with laughter. Sarah doesn't generally use a script and tends to improvise, instilling laughter as she leads with her imagination. Rachael prefers to follow step-by-step instructions, so she knows exactly what to do and what to expect. Once she has seen the game in action, she can put her own twist on it to create new games. We've incorporated samples of both ways of thinking below, so you can find what works best for you.

Sarah's Way . . .

Put on Your Magic Laughter Shoes

How are they magic? These shoes tickle your feet. Maybe your shoes let you fly or hop or jump. Giggle as the shoes begin to tickle you. Walk and laugh in different ways. Bounce! March! Laugh! Swing your hands up and down. Wave your hands as you laugh in slow motion. Chuckle while you skip. Stomp and laugh as you squish the giggles. Wander aimlessly and laugh silently. These prompts are meant to get your feet dancing with imaginary chuckles as you experience your shoes from a variety of perspectives.

Revisit Your Shoes

Pick up a work shoe. Imagine it's a football in your capable hands. Run it down for a touchdown to win the Super Bowl. A ballet slipper, when you take it out of its box, becomes a crying baby you rock to sleep with your soft giggles. A stiletto heel becomes a hammer enabling you to give your kitchen a makeover. You get the idea.

Rachael's Way . . .

LAUGHTER GAME

Laughter-Infused Boots

1. Don your favorite pair of hiking boots with thick ticklish socks as you prepare for a mountain trek.
2. As you begin to feel tired, the boots sense your low energy and stimulate you to release endless belly laughs which put a spring in your step.
3. Every time you stop for a water break, your boot laces dance a jig. Everyone on the path looks on with amazement and laughs in disbelief.
4. At the end of the hike, as you clean and put the boots away, you hear them quietly chuckling as they rest up for your next big climbing adventure.

LAUGHTER GAME

Shoe Shopping with Laughter

Picture yourself in a luxury shoe store. Every type of shoe imaginable is laid out before you: cowboy boots, galoshes, ballet slippers, tap-dancing shoes, cleats, penny loafers, diamond-studded flipflops, stiletto heels, snowshoes, moccasins, hiking boots, snorkeling fins, clogs, extravagant slippers, and imported Italian leather shoes.

1. The shopkeeper brings you a pair of shoes. Try them on.
2. As you saunter, walk, strut, prance, or clomp around the store—LAUGH.
3. Experiment with the nuances of volume, rhythm, and tone in your laughter.
4. Be sure to engage other shoppers in your shoe selection as you inspire them to laugh, too.
5. Ask someone to try on your favorite pair so you can see what they look like on someone else.
6. When the other shopper decides to purchase the shoes you had chosen, burst into laughter as you buy the shoes for them.
7. Erupt into belly laughs as you walk out of the store, and gift all but your favorite pair to delighted strangers.
8. Save the last pair for an aspiring Olympic athlete who will win a gold medal because of your generosity.

Sarah's Twist on Laughing with Shoes

Act out new combinations when you put cowboy boots on for a black-tie wedding. Attend a baseball game in ballet slippers. How would you act at a job interview for a CEO position wearing flip-flops? Remember you can pantomime different scenarios to your heart's content. If you can imagine it, you can laugh with it.

Stimulating Creative Juices

If creativity and imagination seem just out of reach, try some of Rachael's techniques. Her first go-to is—can you guess? Research! You read that correctly. When you have a large knowledge base to draw from, you can often find some little tidbit to inspire new ideas to help you get started. If research isn't your thing, use all kinds of pictures to stimulate out-of-the-box thinking. If you still seek novel ideas, as in this shoe exercise, turn to lists of active verbs to describe different movements. Then match unlikely counterparts, like galloping with a pair of snowshoes or strutting while wearing moccasins. The improbable sets can stimulate some laughter and hopefully tickle your funny bone.

As long as judgment is suspended, play is present. When you bring a willingness to rattle off lots of ideas until one sticks, you'll discover all kinds of gems in your search for laughable connections. We often find that when we bounce ideas off each other, the collaboration leads us to places we could not have found alone.

Mismatch Mayhem

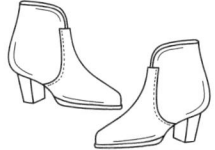

Saunter into an upscale restaurant

Strut into a nursing shift

Take a hike up a snowy mountain

March up creaky stairs

Chase after twin toddlers

Run a marathon

Have fun pairing different actions with a variety of shoes.

SUMMARY: STEPS TO UNLEASH CREATIVITY

Choose an object.
    Infuse the object with magical qualities.
    Transform the object into something new.

Switch the settings or characters.
    Experiment.
    Add movement and play.

Use research and/or visual aids to unlock creativity.

A-muse Yourself

A muse ignites creativity, passion, and inspiration. Let's see what we can find to spark laughter. When you are a-mused, you look through the lens of a kaleidoscope at ordinary occurrences and see new things.

Food

Walk into your kitchen. Let breakfast time become a treasure hunt for inspired giggles and chuckles. While you cook eggs, look for smiles and listen for chuckles as they sizzle. Notice the egg yolks smiling at you. Pour syrup on fluffy pancakes and imagine each bite covered in giggles. Feel them expanding as you chew and swallow. Whatever your breakfast choice, find the joy and gobble it up.

Lunchtime—what's in the sandwich? Tap into your clever genius to include different flavors of laughter as you prepare and consume a nourishing midday meal. Snacks from the cupboard can be sprinkled with chuckles. As you prepare dinner, dance as you dice the vegetables, cackle at the corn, roar with laughter at the roast beef.

Laughter Feast

Prepare a laughter feast. Set the table with color-coordinated laughter. Open your refrigerator. Got citrus, potatoes, or carrots? So many peels. Like *peals* of laughter . . . get it? *HA-HA-HA!*

It may not be so funny. But remember, nothing needs to be funny to laugh! *HO-HO-HO!*

Be on the lookout for a-musing opportunities. Use your newly acquired skills to create unique a-musements and generate lots of joyful laughter.

Travel

Yield to your Inner Child on the road as you travel. Turn on the radio. Become a child again. Laugh and sing along with a song. Music is a delightful complement to laughter and may lead to dancing, too. Let yourself go. Find yourself stuck in traffic? Let chortles, guffaws, and belly laughs move things along. Don't forget Smile-Ups! Laugh yourself silly when you discover a detour. Hop a bus, a train, a plane, or a boat—is it a rowboat or a yacht? Giggle at the thought of each. When you arrive home, put up your feet and relax after a deep round of belly laughs and a rowdy *Very Good, Very Good, YAY!*

Keep Generating New Ideas and Laughter

As long as you're laughing, it doesn't matter if it's in response to humor or from your imagination or one of these generative games. As you laugh more intentionally and with increased frequency, ideas will pop into your mind like popcorn. Train your mind to look around for opportunities. Say to yourself, "How can I respond to this with laughter?" Amplify your creativity. Don't hold back. Watch your mood become more positive as you laugh or as you simply think about it. Don't be surprised if you experience laughter *aftershocks* even weeks after the fun images from these games pop into your mind, reminding you to start strutting and laughing.

Sprinkle Your Memories with Laughter Solutions

Memorable stories are made of unexpected twists and turns when life doesn't go as planned or desired. You can learn to laugh along with chance happenings and look for elements that will at least give you an entertaining story to tell when it's all over.

Flat Tire?

Imagine your flat tire has a face. Smile at the tire as you implore the tire to cooperate. Chuckle at the spare as you coax it to attach easily. Keep your AAA card handy just in case! When the wait is way too long, flag down a truck driver who turns out to be your high school sweetheart. When a picnic lunch is offered after the tire is fixed, share a round of cackles as you reminisce. Do a bit of gratitude laughter as soon as you are safely back on the road. Remember, whatever happens, you have a choice—to laugh or to cry. We heartily recommend laughter. It makes for a better story.

Seeking Comfort

If you have a broken air conditioner during a heat wave, imagine a hand-held fan that generates giggles along with a gentle breeze. Hearty laughter may warm you up, but you can imagine drops of perspiration are giggle ice cubes sent to cool you off. If the power goes out mid-winter, warm your innards with chortles and guffaws as you wrap yourself in belly laughs.

Toss What Doesn't Work

If you are still struggling to generate laughter with these games, don't judge yourself harshly. You may need to loosen up with humor or find a playmate. You may even find laughing with a friend at something you both find funny is your most effective *Jump Start*. Don't give up. Allow your imagination to take flight. Modify or embellish the games as you face new struggles and inconveniences. Keep laughter within easy reach. We have more techniques ahead to help you.

"A good laugh heals
a lot of hurts."

Madeleine L'Engle, Author

Seven

Commit to a Lifetime of Laughter

Life is messy. There's a season for everything. As it says in Ecclesiastes 3:4, "A time to weep and a time to laugh..."

Expressing joy may not be easy or even possible when bad things happen or when you are experiencing deep emotional or physical pain. Yet, it is specifically in those times that we need laughter the most. Ever-increasing and pent-up emotions can turn you into a pressure cooker. Laughter is an incredible release valve that helps restore balance.

If you see a person in pain, laughing is usually the last thing you'd think to offer. Surprisingly, the act of laughing itself can help you through the hard stuff. Even the *really* hard stuff. When Sarah laughed with her daughter Jacqueline, *Jacqueline* initiated the laughter simply by being a child with joy at her fingertips. What about somebody who *doesn't* have immediate access to joy?

The *Laughter Games* in this chapter were created as responses to real problems of our own or requests from clients to help them deal with specific challenges. Because we know the act of laughing changes our brain chemistry, we are committed to offering laughter as a first line of defense for sadness and pain.

If you've ever walked the halls of a convalescent hospital or a hospice care center, laughter is not what you typically hear. In Sarah's laughter coaching, she's had the privilege of working with families and caregivers who are present at the end of life. Laughter can create precious memories for loved ones. When things are hard—*really* hard—laughing is not just possible, it's advisable. It is necessary, even vital.

The Power to Choose

When we know we can't change the circumstances, Irving Berlin's message, "Life is 10% what happens to you and 90% how you respond," resonates. Laughter can help you activate your 90%. Think of this book as a rest stop where you can practice your new superpower of managing life's smaller stresses with a smile and a laugh. Eventually, we hope you'll be able to use these tools for bigger problems.

How do you move from upset to laughter? One useful tool is to think of crossing the street and using the old familiar rule: STOP, LOOK, & LISTEN! Let's apply it to purposefully laughing out loud.

STOP the Madness: Wait a While ~ Pause

While you may not be ready to initiate laughter, checking in with yourself will help laughter weave its magic. Considering laughter as a response will often trigger more positive thoughts. Smiling as you think about and imagine hearing laughter can begin to shift your body's chemicals and stop or slow down the production of cortisol as you ready yourself for laughing.

Sometimes, you're just feeling grim, unhappy, or even mad. Those are times when tapping into humor is a good idea. When Rachael knew she needed to laugh, but doubted she had what it took to chuckle or belly laugh out loud on her own yet, she listened to a routine, *Don't Send a Man to the Grocery Store,* by comedian Jeanne Robertson. Rachael's face hurt from laughing so hard for several minutes. She also felt energized with positive feelings for over an hour!

Check out the following spirited game Rachael created on the spot during a Zoom laughter session when one of her participants reported feeling grim. She had been widowed several months before and was overwhelmed. Rachael wondered how she could help the woman shift from feeling "grim" to smiling and maybe even laughing. "Picture the letters in the word GRIM. How about we rearrange them? Let's turn *GRIM*... into GRIN!" Rachael suggested.

LAUGHTER GAME

Grin & Bear It, or... The Grim Grin Trim

1. Picture the word *GRIM* in your mind.
2. See the letter *M*? Change the *M* to *N*... and you get *GRIN!!!*
3. Now, wipe the *grim* off your face—and put on a *grin* instead.
4. For extra chuckles, repeat *Grim Grin Trim* 3x as fast as you can.

Spoiler alert: tongue twisters are often much harder than they seem. Bet you can't do this one without laughing out loud.

Start by choosing to be silly. Grinning and even laughing through your problems *is* possible. When life presents you with obstacles, practice putting on a grin—even if you don't feel like it. The important thing to remember is that, just as joy can precipitate a grin, a grin can precipitate joy! It works both ways! This is what Rachael used during her breast biopsy in Chapter 3. Even in a dire moment, allowing yourself a momentary lapse into laughter can take you out of your pain. Like Sarah's experience in the hospital, when the laughter subsides, the problem may not look and feel quite so grim. While Rachael's participant couldn't belly laugh right away, she did report feeling lighter by the end of the fifteen-minute laughter session.

LOOK Both Ways: Behind You and Ahead of You

Glasses are used to sharpen our focus when things are fuzzy. Laughter Glasses don't just help you see more clearly and improve your perspective on what's ahead, they help bring you into the present moment. Here's how to uplift yourself and the people around you.

LAUGHTER GAME

Put on Your Laughter Glasses

1. When you're feeling stressed, circle your fingers around your eyes, as if you're holding binoculars.
2. The glasses blur everything and instantly tickle you.
3. Laugh out loud. Laugh at what is stressing you out. Yes . . . *laugh at it!!!*
4. With your laughter glasses, you can laugh at anything. YOU are in control.

After you've worn one pair of laughter glasses, change it up. Shape your fingers into tiny circles, thin slits, fat slits, a monocle, telescopic zoom glasses, fisheye glasses . . . or a microscope. As you pair a different laughter sound with each of the spectacles, see your problem from a unique perspective.

While sporting your imaginary laughter glasses, collect chuckles and stuff giggles and titters into your pockets. You're not crazy. Just driven to succeed. The more you collect in the morning, the more you'll have to give away throughout the day. Keep your eyes open to capture the perfect laughter photographs of people laughing alone or in groups. Share images to inspire others to smile and laugh. Imagine the stimulating conversations your uplifting pictures will spark.

Isn't this intriguing? For extra hoots try saying: *Grim Glasses, Grin Glasses, Trim Glasses.* Repeat multiple times as fast as you can. We double-dog dare you to get the words perfectly three times in a row without rolling on the floor laughing. When you accomplish it, give yourself a *Whoot, whoot!*

Here's an added bonus: Clean the lenses of your Laughter Glasses—now you will see expressions of joy around every corner. If your situation is too challenging and this game won't work for you right now, see if you can don a special pair of glasses to give you a new vantage point.

LISTEN— Make Some Noise!

How? When life throws you a curveball, respond out loud with, "How interesting!" By remaining open to listening, you're creating a path lined with curiosity, learning, and discovery. If your Inner Critic shows up, remember, you're the boss and you can take charge.

Shifting Your Mindset

Negative self-talk often stops us from being positive and playful. The Inner Critic kills laughter.

Go ahead, demote your Inner Critic. She or he likes to whine. We like to muffle the voice of the Inner Critic by surrounding her with uproarious laughter. Sometimes it's easier to soothe her with a song. Turn on the radio and sing along. Lose yourself in the tune. Grab an imaginary microphone and belt out your favorite song to drown out the negativity, or create a playlist for when you need to turn up the volume and eclipse your tendency to find fault with yourself. You might find it useful, as Rachael has, to put up some post-it notes to remind yourself of your favorite upbeat song. As you sing, powerfully reset your thoughts to something playful and uplifting. Rachael uses:

Allow yourself to move from singing to playing. Add motion for extra fun while you laugh and sing. You may want to transform your microphone into a ticklish feather. For an additional twist, bring out your laughter hand-puppets.

> LAUGHTER GAME

The Inner Critic Meets the Laughter Lover

1. Turn your hands into puppets. Open and close your hands as they talk to each other.
2. One hand is your Inner Critic. The other is your Laughter Lover who surrounds negativity with laughter.
3. Speak using your Inner Critic hand puppet. She's a loudmouth!
4. Your laughter-loving hand unleashes an onslaught of laughs. She spreads *giggles*, *chuckles,* and *mirth* all over the Inner Critic, overpowering the whines.
5. Your Inner Critic is so angry. She feels stuck.
6. Reverse the roles of your hand puppets. The Inner Critic hand becomes the Laughter Lover. The Laughter Lover learns to complain. Viewing life from the other's perspective can be valuable.
7. Let both hands complain. Watch as the Laughter Lover emerges from inside each hand. Celebrate yourself for transforming the moment by laughing the complaints away.

Once your Inner Critic is silenced, do a quick mental assessment. Do you have negative thoughts lurking? Let's wash away any lingering clouds of gloom.

LAUGHTER GAME

Cleansing the Negativity

Pantomime holding a huge spray bottle filled with silly suds.
1. Spray everywhere you imagine a gloomy thought is hiding.
2. Laugh with each spritz.
3. Laugh as you wipe away the gloom.
4. Use a squeegee to get rid of every speck of trouble.

Notice in this game we are personifying negativity and gloom and adding play and laughter. This is a powerful way to reshape your thinking. Like cleaning tools, laughter comes in many forms. When you experience a downpour of troubles, scatter them, using energetic windshield wipers of laughter. If you experience a spark from a tricky challenge igniting into a house fire, it's time to haul in the firehose to the rescue. Belly laughs can extinguish the flames, leaving uplifting puddles of giggles behind.

You can choose to laugh on demand. We sometimes need a little coaxing—gentle reminders of our laughter powers. Occasionally we forget we have an innate ability to laugh. Imagine someone tapping on your shoulder. Why? To nudge you to laugh, of course.

LAUGHTER GAME

Who's Tapping On Your Shoulder?

Let's pretend. Imagine someone or something tapping on your shoulder.

1. Whatever you're doing, pause and tap one of your shoulders. Don't stop. It's as if your fingers have a mind of their own.
2. What you see aren't fingers . . . but bouncing giggles! What are *they* doing here? They've come to rescue you from your mounting concerns.
3. No use grumbling at the giggles. You might as well laugh along with them.
4. Surrender to the infectious laughter. Sense the flow of positive energy. For now, laughing banishes worries . . . unless it doesn't.
5. Just for grins, start tapping your other shoulder. Repeat steps 1-4.
6. Once you can sustain a hearty laugh, turn your head back and forth between the two sets of tapping giggles. Are you ready to continue your day? Congratulate yourself for choosing laughter to help you clear your mind.

Notice that implementing laughter at any challenging juncture can turn your whole day around.

How Laughter Can Help with Stress

At times we find ourselves feeling day-to-day stress and overwhelm. In order to eliminate and get rid of the stress altogether, we may need to face the stress head-on and interact with it directly. Purposefully inserting laughter can help free our minds so we can reframe and address any stress.

Grab your imagination and come with us.

Picture your stress as a tangible *thing* you can hold. Your mind is extremely powerful, so we invite you to literally imagine holding *your stress,* like a ball, in your hands. See your helpless feeling as you wait impatiently at the pharmacy to pick up a much-needed prescription for a family member. Think about what makes this specific thing so stressful for you. Allow yourself to fully feel the stress.

And then, as the wait continues . . .

- LAUGH as you stuff your stress ball into a box and tape it shut.
- LAUGH as you mail it to someone in a faraway land.
- LAUGH as you envision the box of your stress arriving at its destination.

When you attempt to remove stress from your life by sharing it, the stress will change.

It gets smaller.
The stress arrives as a much smaller version of what you mailed...

- If you sent a MONSTER, it's now a cute little yipping beastie.
- If you sent the FOG OF DOOM, it melted into a harmless puddle.
- If you sent a TOXIC SPIKE BALL, it's now a smooth and happy bouncy ball.

LAUGH more as you imagine someone opening the box and reacting to the stress you sent. Now take a breath. If you find your own stress returned to you, notice it's been repackaged. With a different look and feel you may be able to cope with it a little better. If you find someone else's stress in your mailbox, rearrange theirs, too, and send it back to them with an encouraging note.

Congratulations, you creatively managed your stress. Or, maybe it didn't work for you. Sometimes you need a more advanced tool to deal with your stress, or your stress sneaks back in on you.

Sarah

Protect Yourself with Laughter

Laughter Shield to the rescue. I've been using some form of laughter protection since I was young. I learned it from the joy of Grandpa Barney. I practiced it regularly each time I decided not to let life get me down. When you've got an eye patch, a back brace, or a very sick child or spouse, it helps to be able to laugh. If you're not quite ready to laugh out loud on your own, a prop may help. Enter the Laughter Shield.

Design Your Laughter Shield

Throughout history, the shield has saved lives and won battles. Ancient Greek soldiers each held a big circular shield called an *aspis* to protect against attack. Ancient Roman soldiers held a long rectangular shield called a *scutum*. Each was used in a different way for unique styles of combat.

When you're disconnected from your source of power, the Laughter Shield allows you to feel safe and take back control. The mere knowledge that you have a shield to offer protection can boost your confidence and sense of security. Safety relieves stress and empowers your thoughts and emotions, restoring your equanimity. Your challenge will determine the type of Laughter Shield you choose. You may need a big one, a thick one, or one with an elaborate design meant to grab your attention and distract you from your troubles.

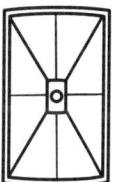  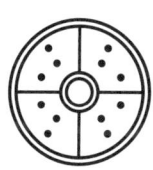 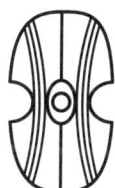

LAUGHTER GAME

Put Up Your Laughter Shield

1. Focus on what feels insurmountable.
2. Visualize yourself holding a powerful shield.
3. Picture the shape, material, designs, and colors. The more magnificent the shield, the more real and powerful it will feel.
4. Hold the shield as a protective barrier directly between you and the trouble.
5. Transform the shield by coating it with robust sounds of laughter, and watch the trouble retreat more rapidly as you increase the power of your laughter.
6. Laugh vigorously at each problem with your shield held firmly in place.

The Laughter Shield in Action

As a laughter professional, I have never been more validated than when I coached Brent, my now ex-husband—a busy lawyer—while in the midst of our divorce. He called me one day from the office. Before I knew it, I found myself coaching him through a tense time. He felt particularly stressed, unable to focus despite looming deadlines and mounting pressures.

In *Laughter Games* we promise to suspend judgment. With self-acceptance and an awareness of the power of laughter in mind, these are the steps I coached him through, with dialogue:

Step 1: Accept the Current Situation

"This may seem strange," I said. "Close your office door and just go with me. Say, 'yes' to whatever is going on, even if you don't like it."

I asked him to say: "Yes, I am at work."

"Yes, I have a lot of pressing deadlines."

"Yes, I am distracted by things going on in my personal life."

"Yes, I have a big new assignment and my promotion depends on it."

"Yes, my chest is tightening, and my breathing is shallow."

"Yes, I feel like screaming."

Step 2: Take a Deep Breath

"Okay," I said. "Let's breathe." I heard him breathe deeply through the phone as he slowly began to exhale and relax.

Step 3: Yes, AND . . .

Then I asked him to say: "Yes, this is what I am dealing with, AND . . . I can smile despite everything. Just a little smile."

I borrowed from the practice of improvisational theater that turns, "No, BUT . . ." into "Yes, AND . . ." I had been using some version of the "Yes, AND . . ." approach for myself and with him for years. Maybe this time he'd hear it differently.

"Okay, Sarah," he said. "Yes, this is what I'm dealing with, AND I can smile despite everything. And yes, I'm smiling."

Step 4: Add Smile-Ups

"Great!" I said. Normally, he laughs pretty easily, yet he's hesitant to experiment with intentional laughter. "Let's expand your smile into a few Smile-Ups." I heard him chuckle. "Can you laugh again?" I asked. He let out another tentative chuckle, and I sensed his defenses beginning to soften.

Step 5: Practice Laughter Breaths

"Let's do some Laughter Breaths," I said. He sighed, but I detected his smile over the phone. His comfort eased as he warmed up for the smallest laugh.

Step 6: Identify the Source of Your Stress

"I have a few questions," I said. "What's the source of your stress?"

"Everything," he said. "My personal life and my work life are both a mess." *As if I didn't know. Of course your life is a mess. Mine is too—we're getting divorced.*

Statistically, we knew that couples who lose a child often end up divorced. Years ago we had sworn to each other we would not add to that statistic. Even as I write these words, I can't tell you exactly what happened, but I couldn't let divorce define me any more than my other life challenges had. I often thought of Grandpa Barney and Jacqueline and knew I would get through this difficult time, too.

I knew helping Brent in that moment would also help me. I rarely shared my stress with him. When he brought his stress home, from whatever source, it infected our space. I recall many people telling me, "This is so unfair. You must be so angry." I felt none of that. Life is not fair or unfair. It just is. Laughter had served me well so far. I determined to keep putting it to work for me during this new challenge.

The Laughter Shield idea immediately came to me: *What can protect you from everything, including yourself? Laughter, of course—it has the power to keep stress at bay.*

Step 7: Use Your Imagination to Create and Position Your Laughter Shield

"So," I said. "I want you to use your imagination. When you feel you can't possibly cope, you need to *shield yourself* from everything causing you stress."

Step 8: Use Your Laughter Shield to Deflect Your Troubles

"Put up an imaginary shield as big as you want. The shield is a wall of laughter that will protect you from your troubles as long as you continue laughing." I encouraged him to visualize the shield and the scene in great detail and to feel the vibration of his own chortles and belly laughs as the shield expanded to protect him.

I felt awkward helping him cope with problems in his personal life. I wondered if I was the source of those problems or if it was something else. Or maybe it was the divorce. I pushed those thoughts away. I took quick note of my own stress and allowed myself to laugh right along with him, with my own Laughter Shield in position.

Step 9: Debrief:

After several minutes of laughing together, we debriefed as I asked him to:

- Take a deep, cleansing breath.
- Check in with his body.
- Notice how he felt.
- Take stock of his energy level.
- Determine his readiness to go back to work.

I wasn't the least surprised when he said: "I can't believe it. This works! I do feel better." He had just laughed through his troubles.

He sent feel-good chemicals—dopamine, oxytocin, serotonin, and endorphins—coursing through his body. He began to feel better after curbing his body's stress response. He expressed relief and readiness to open his door so he could go back to work.

I still smile inside when I think about his transformation. His success gave me great personal satisfaction. Despite the complications and difficulties in our relationship and his life, I managed to coach him through an especially challenging day. I knew he trusted me and likely felt awkward and vulnerable sharing his feelings right then. I also knew laughter has the power to break down barriers. We both felt more connected and energized after the shared laughs. I was sure his feelings about purposeful laughter were forever altered.

NOT SO FUN FACT

Burnout

None of us is alone in suffering from work-related stress. According to statistics from the American Institute of Stress, nearly 83% of workers in the United States experience work-related stress.[20]

---

20 Caitlin Mazur, "40+ Worrisome Workplace Stress Statistics [2023]: Facts, Causes, And Trends," Zippia.com. Feb. 11, 2023. https://www.zippia.com/advice/workplace-stress-statistics/.

LAUGHTER SHIELD SUMMARY

Step 1: Accept the situation by saying, "Yes" to whatever is going on, even if you don't like it.

Step 2: Take a deep breath.

Step 3: Accept your current situation as it is and realize the choices and power you *do* have by saying, "Yes, AND . . . "

Step 4: Add Smile-Ups.

Step 5: Add Laughter Breaths.

Step 6: Identify the source of your stress.

Step 7: Use your imagination to create and position your Laughter Shield.

Step 8: Use your Laughter Shield to deflect your troubles.

Step 9: Debrief:

    Take a cleansing breath.

    Do a full body scan as you focus on relaxing.

    Notice your energy level and how you feel.

"Trouble knocked at the door, but, hearing laughter, hurried away."

Benjamin Franklin, Founding Father, United States of America

Eight

Use Laughter to Cope and Succeed

Do you have a support system to help you cope with life's challenges? Smiles, giggles, and chuckles are effective to help us deal with the curveballs we face. There are ups and downs in life for everyone. Whether we're facing the trials of raising children, negative environments, personal illness, relationship tests, or striving for success, positivity is an essential tool for effective coping. Because laughter generates powerful chemicals, adding laughter to manage our challenges is a handy habit worth cultivating. We encourage you to familiarize yourself with this coping strategy.

Early in her research about laughter, Rachael discovered laughter therapist, Annette Goodheart, and her book, *Laughter Therapy, How to Laugh About Everything in Your Life That Isn't Really Funny*. Rachael was thrilled to read that laughter causes whole-body relaxation and sometimes results in tension-easer pee for lots of people. Goodheart described her own experiences with it. "Since I started doing Laughter work publicly, I have started wearing skirts... panty liners are very helpful to stem [any] embarrassment."[21] Reading about Goodheart lifted some of Rachael's humiliation and shame. She felt her confidence being restored.

Goodheart also made a convincing case for laughing out loud and losing control, when she explained her approach: It's not about control, "It is about helping ourselves laugh... laughing for no reason, laughing when we are not happy, and laughing when nothing is 'funny.' The paradox is that by losing control through laughter, we gain control of our lives in flexible, intelligent, creative, and caring ways... and have a whale of a good time."[22] Her words drew Rachael in because she deeply yearned to experience the combination of control and fun Goodheart spoke about while steering her life in the direction she wanted to go.

Life is often unpredictable. We have repeatedly found that when we put purposeful, playful laughter to work for us, we seize control while having fun, just as Goodheart describes.

Laughing When Sick

Whether you're visiting a sick friend or feeling under the weather yourself, laughter can lift your spirits as it sets the stage for healing. Sometimes sickness may be so great that laughter isn't physically possible without employing other

---

21 Annette Goodheart, PhD, *Laughter Therapy: How to Laugh About Everything in Your Life That Isn't Really Funny* (Santa Barbara: Less Stress Press, 1994), 74.

22 Goodheart, *Laughter Therapy*, 36.

forms of medicine first. A person in a coma or on a ventilator can't laugh. A person with nausea, or doubled over and vomiting, can't laugh. But for the most part, if you are well enough to breathe and think on your own, you are well enough to participate in some sort of laughter.

Laughter helps alleviate pain and sends stress on a hike. Even a sick person can be distracted by the sounds of laughter regardless of the severity of the illness.

Here are a few ways you can creatively bring laughter to a friend, relative, or even yourself:

- Laugh as you give your internal organs a full-on laughter massage.
- Laugh as you smear 'laughter lotion' on someone's sick and tired parts.
- Laugh as you swallow a handful of giggles.

As you prepare to visit a sick friend, you want to be sensitive and say or do the right thing. Here are some tips:

- Start with a genuine smile. You don't need words. Someone with low energy will usually return a smile.
- Let your smile become a gentle laugh. They will appreciate your giggles.
- You can teach Smile-Ups to the sick patient and invite them to be your Smile Buddy.
- Remember, just the sound of your laughter will be uplifting.

LAUGHTER GAME

Gentle Finger Laughter

This easy finger *Laughter Game* evokes joy and laughter. When you or your friend need a pick-me-up, use your fingers to shift your mindset and emotions to stimulate energy. Finger laughter may be particularly suitable because it requires minimum exertion.

1. Put your hands together in front of your body, palms touching, fingers spread wide.
2. Separate your thumbs and then gently bring them back together, as if they were clapping, and say, *Ha!*
3. Repeat and add more fingers. Clap your thumbs quickly followed by clapping your index fingers and say, *Ha-Ha!* (One *Ha!* for each clap.)
4. Continue—clap the thumbs, the index fingers, and add a new finger in the sequence each time until all five fingers have been included in the group laugh, *Ha-Ha-Ha-Ha-Ha*, with five mini claps.
5. Move all your fingers back and forth as you enthusiastically laugh, *Ha-Ha-Ha-Ha-Ha*, each time your fingertips touch.
6. Reverse the finger clapping. Start with the pinkie fingers and move toward the thumbs.
7. Speed up. Go faster and faster until you can't stop laughing. Don't worry if you mess up. You simply can't get it wrong. After all, you're laughing!

Caregiver Laughter

Sarah arrived early to a charitable event hosted by her friend, Anna. She immediately sensed something beyond pre-event jitters. Hours earlier, Anna and her husband, Massimo, sat across from their doctor who explained in a slow and steady voice, "Massimo has stage IV gastric cancer."

Sarah took Anna aside and gave her a long hug. Looking into Anna's eyes she said, "You *must* do these three things:

1. Take care of yourself every single day. Do something to nourish your body and spirit. Before you can be available to tend to someone else, you must first nurture yourself.
2. Learn everything you can about what is going on so you can make the best decisions.
3. Find ways to play and celebrate together. Use music, nature, creative arts—it doesn't matter—just keep making memories.

Anticipating Anna and her husband would be reluctant to ask for help, Sarah offered to come over the next day to laugh with them. They accepted. They started with Smile-Ups and finger skipping and built up to big belly laughs. After forty-five minutes of continuous play and laughter, the three of them found relief. Sarah had modeled how to use laughter to de-stress and lighten their load, to bolster them for the rocky road ahead. She joined them in Italy, Massimo's homeland, where they went for his treatment, to offer laughter and support.

End-of-Life Laughter

Over the years, hospice nurses have consulted Sarah about *Laughter Games*. They understand the value of intentional laughter, both for themselves as caregivers, and for their palliative care patients.

Sarah's involvement in every aspect of Jacqueline's care is in her mind when she speaks with nurses. The advice she gave Anna came from her own personal experience. While taking care of Jacqueline, Sarah learned to prioritize her needs so she could recharge and stay fresh. She teaches caregivers how to use laughter tools to remain positive, and to picture themselves healthy while doing things they love, so they can be at their best for their patients, their families, and themselves.

Just as most people feel rejuvenated after a beach trip, many feel the same benefit after laughing. Laughter can be as powerful as a trip to your favorite vacation spot, while infinitely more available. This is a huge boon for hospice patients, who usually aren't mobile. Sarah created something fun and accessible for them, using simple finger *Laughter Games*.

LAUGHTER GAME

Childhood Memories at the Beach

1. Pretend your fingers are your feet and run playfully to the water.
2. Pull your arms close to your body as your finger-feet curl into fists to simulate jumping back from the water's edge in time to avoid a big wave.
3. Continue approaching the water and jumping back a few times, laughing with abandon until you feel brave enough to jump in and start swimming.
4. Ready? Dive in! Not with your fingers, but with YOU. Your whole self.
5. Use your arms to swim out to sea. Let laughter escape as you vigorously swim further and further.
6. Shark! Laugh at it. Quick, do the backstroke with your arms, as fast as you can, but keep laughing to escape.
7. Relax your shoulders. Breathe as you return to safety on the sandy beach.

Sarah has played this game many times. Her most memorable moment came as she laughed with a hospice patient surrounded by family and caregivers. At the conclusion of the game the patient let out an unexpected *Very Good, Very Good, YAY!* Quite by accident, her hands came to rest on her blanket, curled in the shape of a heart. When her daughter saw her heart-shaped hands, she beamed with joy—what a powerful Mother's Day memory.

Sarah

Laughing Through COVID

Believe it or not, laughing every day can pull you from a deep abyss. That's exactly what I experienced in 2020 during the COVID-19 pandemic. I was decluttering my Minneapolis house where I'd lived for twenty-five years, preparing to put it on the market. My daughter Allison was soon to be married in New York. I was making travel plans and coordinating events for friends and family from around the world.

Then COVID happened. Everything locked down.

In just days, Allison's wedding was postponed. My house was taken off the market. All our plans were turned upside down because of travel bans and gathering restrictions. As you can imagine, it was a big disappointment. Being a laughter coach, I forced myself to chuckle. I hoped I would find a way to keep others laughing, too. Certainly, nothing *seemed* funny.

And yet, here was serendipity: Allison and her fiancé left their one-bedroom, New York apartment and headed to the Midwest to live with *me* for an undetermined period of time.

As uncertainty and fear of the pandemic gripped the world, I became aware of a potent, yet unspoken need to ease the tension. I knew we all needed to laugh.

That's when I hosted my first virtual laughter session on Facebook Live. I shared twenty minutes of laughter with whoever clicked in. I quickly discovered helping others wasn't the only benefit. As I committed to share laughter at the same time every day, I realized how much *I* needed it. Sometimes we don't notice we are in the grip of fear or isolation until we begin to feel more connected to the same emotions in others.

My public commitment to laugh every day gave my life structure and meaning. After a full seven days of sharing laughter, I started to relax. My mood was lighter. Fears had dissipated. No longer did I feel anxiety or worry lodged in the pit of my stomach. Looking back, I can't imagine how my life would have looked after COVID if I had not consciously and literally laughed my way through it.

Teaching people to laugh helped me shift focus from myself to making a difference for others. Laughter might not be the cure for COVID-19, but for those in my laughter group, laughing out loud together *was* the cure for a lot of the stress, pain, and loneliness created by the pandemic.

Reassurance and Encouragement

In the early days of the pandemic, one of our laughter colleagues, Mike Forester, introduced us to something he was finding useful to boost people's spirits. Everything's **G**onna **B**e **O**-**K**ay! (EGBOK!) became a fun and positive *Laughter Game* in his hands. We began incorporating the uplifting chant of EGBOK! with our own twist into our laughter sessions as a universal message of hope. Add EGBOK! to your day.

LAUGHTER GAME

EGBOK!

1. Clap as you say, *EGBOK! EGBOK! BOK! BOK! BOK!* (Repeat 3X)
2. Continue clapping as you say, *Everything's Gonna Be O-Kay!*
3. Keep clapping and say, *Be O-Kay! Be O-Kay! Be O-Kay!*
4. Again clap and say, *Everything's Gonna Be O-Kay!*
5. Now, squawk like a chicken, flap your arms with the sounds, *BOK! BOK! BOK! BOK! BOK!* until you start cackling. You can even *BOK!* while you're laughing.
6. End with a resounding, *Everything's Gonna Be O-Kay!*
7. Throw your arms up in the air, saying *EGBOK!* one last time.

Washing your hands for a full twenty seconds with soap and water helps fight infection and prevent disease. To make hand washing for twenty seconds a healthy habit, Sarah created a *Laughter Game* called WYHa20 (pronounced Wee-Ha 20) which stands for **W**ash **Y**our **Ha**nds for **20** seconds. In this game we laugh at the disappearing germs for the doctor-recommended twenty seconds. Think of spreading soap suds, joy, and giggles in place of germs. Read through the directions first, then set a timer for twenty seconds when you're ready to begin.

LAUGHTER GAME

WYHa20

1. Pantomime washing your hands and add different laughter sounds throughout.
2. Lather with laughter, remembering to wash between your fingers.
3. Wash your wrists and clean your nails, too. Pretend you are a surgeon prepping for surgery.
4. When you finish or when the timer rings, let out a *Wheee Haaaaa!*
5. If you need encouragement along the way, say, *Whee Haaaa!* with added chuckles throughout the game.

Cultivate Flexibility

We are often called upon to adapt to changes in life. Each of us wears a unique collection of hats: caregiver, breadwinner, teacher, master chef, and so much more.

Elite athletes have mastered their ability to recover from errors or distractions quickly. They pivot well and are thus ready to make their next move and perform at their best. We, too, can harness the same ability when we have to switch or manage multiple tasks simultaneously. Laughter is the best tool we know to prepare to pivot and respond optimally to changes. To play this game, move quickly and rely on your imagination.

LAUGHTER GAME

The Perfect Pivot

1. Imagine yourself in an irritating situation. Strike a pose that places you in the center of whatever is happening.
2. Instead of scowling or furrowing your brow at your irritation, laugh heartily.
3. PIVOT. Assume a different stance. As you move, choose a different situation and a new laughter sound. Hold the pose for at least fifteen seconds as you continue to laugh.
4. PIVOT again. Rearrange your pose and laugh differently, reframing your latest challenge both physically and mentally.

After you have pivoted at least five times, give yourself an enthusiastic congratulatory laugh for well-executed plays. Notice creative problem-solving thoughts emerge as your perspective changes with each new pose.

Shift with Gratitude

If you need a boost to start laughing, practice elevating your emotional state with gratitude. When you move your thoughts to gratitude, appreciation can reveal the hidden silver lining on dark hovering clouds. When laughter doesn't feel readily available, consciously looking for miracles and finding the gifts that surround us can elicit feelings of joy.

When Sarah was going through her divorce, she recalled how many people had said that she and Brent seemed to have the perfect relationship. She thought they regularly modeled give-and-take for their daughters who she hoped would one day have their own successful marriages. It was mind-boggling to unravel how and when what seemed so good had fallen apart.

During that time, Sarah often found it difficult to summon even the simplest chuckle, despite knowing she'd feel better after laughing. Gratitude came easier. The perfection of a flower always left her full of awe.

Allow yourself to feel grateful to be alive and able to witness so much beauty in the natural world. We hope feeling grateful will put a smile on your face, and with time, enable you to generate some giggles.

LAUGHTER GAME

Gratitude Laughter

1. Create a mental list of people and things you are grateful for and want to acknowledge. Keep your list in mind for the duration of the game.
2. Bring your hands to your heart.
3. Inhale as you breathe in gratitude.
4. Close your eyes and visualize the people, places, and things on your list.
5. As you exhale, stretch your arms wide and fling gratitude, love, and laughter far into the universe.
6. Visualize the people you've thought about truly receiving your heartfelt emotions.
7. Repeat the movements. With love, inhale gratitude, exhale laughter.

Bonus Giggle Opportunity

Call one of the people you just acknowledged and ask them if they received the gratitude you sent. Contacting them to share your admiration and appreciation enhances your connection and gives you both an extra special boost. Be sure to laugh together.

Don't be surprised if you suddenly cry. Laughter and tears spring from the same emotional place and provide a cleansing and rejuvenating release. Say *YES!* to life. Don't judge yourself. Feel joy wash over you in the wake of gratitude. Even in the midst of suffering, you can still find glorious reasons to celebrate as you focus on what you appreicate in life.

Author Stephen King said, "You can't deny laughter; it plops down in your favorite chair and stays as long as it wants." We think gratitude works the same way. When you fill your heart with gratitude its warmth embraces you like a cozy blanket.

Laughter Plays a Role in Success

People we've laughed with in our workshops have shared that laughing has built up their confidence, raised their self-esteem, and led to more creative problem-solving. Laughter helps lower inhibitions and allows us to shift our perspectives. Many report feeling more optimistic and more motivated after a good laugh. Improvements in alertness, memory recall, creativity, and even altruism have also been attributed to regular robust laughter. Andrew Carnegie, one of the richest men in America and a big philanthropist, understood the power of laughter. He said, "There is little success where there is little laughter."

Rachael has experienced several of these benefits herself. After becoming a Laughter Yoga leader, Rachael ventured out and tentatively led a laughter session for older adults. She was surprised that laughter came so easily to them, and she remained uplifted long after the session ended. She was caught off-guard when one of the attendees, years later, offered her a job based on the joy and energy they had experienced in that early session.

Og Mandino, best-selling author of *The Greatest Salesman in the World*, created a system for success, designed to replace a lifetime of bad habits with good ones in ten months. His mantra was "This too shall pass." He didn't allow failure or a lot of *No's* to get him down. He created ten principles for success, the seventh one being "I will laugh at the world." He declared, "Henceforth I will cultivate the habit of laughter. I will smile and my digestion will improve; I will chuckle and my burdens will be lightened. I will laugh and my life will be lengthened, for this is the great secret of long life and now it is mine."[23] It's like the Irish saying: "A good laugh and a long sleep are the two best cures for anything."

We think Mandino had the right idea. Stress can lead to a large variety of illnesses and physical problems. It disrupts our ability to focus and to achieve our goals. Stress impacts every social interaction. Imagine how different life would be if we all adopted Mandino's approach. Smiles and chuckles would replace grumbling and curmudgeonly behavior.

We seek and pursue laughter for the joy it expresses and all the benefits it bestows upon us when we are ready to indulge and partake of its gifts, both inwardly and outwardly. The more frequently you laugh intentionally, the more masterful

---

23   Og Mandino, *The Greatest Salesman in the World* (New York: Bantam Books, 1968), 83-87.

you'll become at laughing. As you celebrate finishing this chapter, let's acknowledge your accomplishments together.

> **LAUGHTER GAME**
>
> # Celebrate Your Accomplishments Laugh
>
> We're giving you a standing ovation.
>
> 1. Take a bow.
> 2. Do a victory lap.
> 3. Strike a body-building pose. Look in the mirror if you can.
> 4. Change your pose several times as you laugh. Be sure to acknowledge yourself as you move.
> 5. Breathe deeply and decide to incorporate even more laughter into your life.
>
> Bravo, for a job well done! *Very Good, Very Good, YIPPEE!*

As we regain our composure following *Laughter Games* we carry the glow back into our lives. Once you practice consistent playful laughter, finding excuses for ecstatic rejoicing will become second nature. Now let's make it a habit.

"Motivation is what gets you started, habit is what keeps you going."

Jim Ryun, Olympic Athlete

Nine

Establish a Laughter Habit

Establishing routines is helpful when accomplishing our goals. When you plan to initiate a new behavior pattern, practicing regularly will help ensure it becomes second nature. When a consciously established behavior becomes your new natural response to a given situation, you're well on your way to success! In this chapter, we will show you steps to create powerful laughter habits as we infuse each day with fun.

Sometimes we suddenly realize we need a new habit. Let's say you've just suffered a heart attack. *Yikes!* You're scared. You've never been more committed to your health and will do anything your doctor says. Well, maybe not *anything*.

If Dr. Michael Miller, the cardiologist we mentioned in Chapter 4, were your heart doctor, he would write you a prescription for fifteen minutes of belly laughs every day.

What? He wants me to laugh every day? Is he serious? Hmmmmm . . . Interesting . . . Compelling. But having a heart attack or facing bypass surgery is no time to laugh. I'm a busy person with a family depending on me. How on earth will I fill fifteen minutes a day with laughter? And how many doctors talk about laughing, anyway? Shouldn't I be taking medications, eating right, exercising . . . and getting a second opinion PRONTO!?

Of course, doctor-prescribed medication, diet, and exercise are important. It's natural to respond to a dire situation with fear, which triggers stress. It is exactly that stressful moment that calls for inserting self-generated laughter so you can bring yourself back into balance. The first step to establishing a laughter habit is having the willingness and even enthusiasm to build it.

Do you laugh every day? Not everyone does. Rachael sure didn't. There were times when Rachael desperately wanted to laugh, but the sounds she made felt weak and false. She didn't like the awkward, throaty, and fake sound of her own laugh. Rachael had a vision of the payoff in her mind—becoming more laid back and fun to be around—but she was having trouble getting there.

"Just let go and laugh!" Sarah cajoled her and reminded Rachael to stop judging herself. Coaxing her Inner Child out to play was tough. Rachael was comfortable skipping—it always triggered smiles in the past—so she practiced skipping around the living room and around the cul-de-sac. She added finger laughter and gave herself permission to watch silly videos. Even though Sarah's goal was to teach Rachael to laugh freely at will, pedaling along on the training wheels of external triggers, like humor, was useful to get Rachael going.

Creating a New Identity

Identity struggles were very familiar to Rachael. She subconsciously created an identity that helped her survive, but wasn't serving her highest potential. She participated in a yearlong program called Sati365, run by Patricia Moreno, with a variety of structures to support the fulfillment of whatever goals were set. Patricia offered weekly motivational meetings, accountability groups, daily exercise, regular writing, and a huge quantity of resources. One could often hear Patricia saying, "One percent improvement, one day at a time," and "Progress not perfection." These phrases were repeated and supported the participants in sustaining new routines and habits. Rachael credits this program with motivating her to establish a regular laughter habit and writing this book. She's well on her way to becoming the positive person she wants to share with the world.

Rachael

I made a conscious decision to add more intentional laughter to my life. I wasn't sure how to accomplish it. I took a bold step.

I declared myself a *Laughter Champion!* (Has a nice ring to it, don't you think?)

When you want to change something about yourself, getting clear about the desired outcome is helpful. Taking my favorite pen in hand, I began to create a vision of myself as a more positive, joyful, contagiously laughing person. I liked the sound of a Laughter Champion, but what exactly did that mean? I looked up the word *champion*: one who enthusiastically supports something they believe in. I realized I already regularly promoted purposeful, playful laughter. I saw myself as a flag-bearer for laughter, but I was nothing like a prizewinner or gold medalist when it came to laughing out loud on demand. As I wrote my declaration, line by line, I also imagined myself becoming that new person.

I didn't just say, "I am going to be a Laughter Champion," I described what it would feel like to me and what others would experience if I already embodied this new persona. *What would it be like if I were comfortable smiling and laughing effortlessly every day?* I intended to smile in the mirror every day, consciously keep the benefits of laughing front of mind, and let go of resistance whenever I caught myself shutting down. I expanded my role to include being an Ambassador of Positivity. I was well on my way.

I committed to cultivating a noticeable daily attitude of joy and play. I gave myself clear directions for coping with unwanted, uninvited negativity. I decided to turn judgments into curiosity with a chance to learn and grow, look for reasons to appreciate myself and others, thus pushing pause on pessimism.

After I typed the entire declaration, made it pretty, and laminated it, I stood in front of the mirror and read the whole thing aloud with conviction. As I caught a glimpse of the woman reading my declaration, I noticed my eyes sparkle with a sincere smile and genuine self-love.

Remarkably, no matter how many times I recite the declaration, I feel fresh tingles and renewed inspiration, as if I'm seeing myself anew each time.

Your turn.

Stand in front of a mirror and read my declaration aloud. Feel free to adopt mine or write your own. Vocalize your new commitments with sincerity. Embody the words as you recite. Become The Laughter Champion and Ambassador of Positivity you're describing.

Declaration of a Laughter Champion

*Today I share my **smile**.*

*I engage my eyes and add some **sparkle**.*

*I bring forth love as I share my **smile**.*

*I generate **giggles** as I exhale, mindful of the many benefits of pushing stale air out of my lungs with laughter. I am an **Ambassador of Positivity**.*

*I am **mindful** of the process of releasing my resistance and inviting my Inner Child to remind me how to **play**—with wild abandon and wonder.*

*I bring an attitude of **joy** and **play** to my day.*

*The people I encounter are infected with my **laughter**, feel my **enthusiasm** and **fun**, and share their own energy with others.*

*I am a **Laughter Champion**, the embodiment of **joy**, **positivity**, **play**, **lightness**, and **fun**.*

I bring this state of being into every interaction.

*And when negativity starts to creep in, I will notice, acknowledge the opportunity to practice **shifting**, and with **Laughter Breaths** I will begin to call up the full embodiment of a **Laughter Champion**.*

I will do this for the rest of my life, and be known for the shift in my being.

To help ensure my success, I created my own personal 40-Day Laughter Challenge. I committed to laugh on camera for forty days straight. Fulfilling the public promise changed me.

In the course of doing this challenge, I found as I consciously *chose* to respond to life with laughter—my attitude shifted dramatically. Merely *thinking about laughing* led me to empowering discoveries that continue to motivate and inspire me. I found the desire to laugh pushed me toward a more positive outlook. The choice to respond to life with purposeful, playful laughter still has me on the lookout for fun. The search for optimistic perspectives stretches my gratitude muscles. The creativity and imagination I use while conjuring laughter triggers a cascade of pleasant thoughts and ideas, which in turn stimulate connections, teamwork, trust, creativity, and even intimacy. Further, when I find myself upset, an inner dialogue soon begins between my Inner Critic and my Laughter Guide.

> Inner Critic: "This is frustrating, you don't have time to wait, how disappointing and annoying."

> Laughter Guide: (interrupting with a laugh): "You know better than to let this upset you. You're a Laughter Champion. You'll feel better after a few Smile-Ups and giggles."

Do you notice how the Laughter Guide diverted the Inner Critic away from the annoying situation and toward fulfilling my role as a Laughter Champion? The Laughter Guide has the same effect on *me* as laughter has on shutting down the production of *cortisol*.

From my own first-hand experience, I learned laughter really is empowering.

Turn a Bad Habit into a Good One with Play

We each have our pet peeves, and one of my husband's is when lights get left on in our house.

My growing laughter habit helped me overcome my increasing irritation with his seemingly incessant reminders to turn off this or that light. Sometimes it seemed petty. *Ok, so I left a light on, so what?* With my annoyance meter rising fast, I quickly moved to get to the light switch before he did. I often got there first.

I hated being reminded about the lights. My Inner Critic made it mean he was annoyed with *me*. This would have been a great opportunity to take out my Laughter Shield, put on my Laughter Glasses, or chant my way out using EGBOK!—**E**verything's **G**onna **B**e **O**-**K**ay! But I didn't yet have these laughter tools at my disposal. What I did have, was play. So I made a game out of it—one we could both win.

I told him I'd give him a quarter every time he caught me leaving a light on if he agreed to do the same every time I caught him. The results were—fun! I caught myself leaving lights on and hurried to turn them off or call myself out before he did, so I could save a quarter. And guess what? Before long, *he* owed me a few quarters. Sometimes I laughed out loud as I scurried to turn the lights off. When we had accumulated enough quarters, we treated ourselves to dinner. We turned a potential conflict into laughter and closeness.

I succeeded in transforming my unconscious (bad) habit of leaving the lights on into a good habit while using playfulness and friendly competition. Not every relationship annoyance can be laughed at while it's happening. With a bit of conscious effort, play, and laughter you may be able to create something new, too. The door is open. Come join us on a quest for a new way of being in your life.

Creating a Laughter Habit

Ready to train your brain to laugh? In his book *Atomic Habits,* James Clear writes: "The ultimate purpose of habits is to solve the problems of life with as little energy and effort as possible."[24] Imagine if you laughed *automatically* in response to things without *thinking* about laughing. How great would that be? For us, intentionally creating laughter as a first response is the embodiment of both Og Mandino's mantra of "this too shall pass" and his commitment to *Laugh with Life*. These skills are key to creating a life of positivity, gratitude, and joy.

How to Build a Habit

James Clear suggests three basic ways to create a new habit.

1. Make a plan—grab your laughter planner.
2. Stack habits.
3. Respond to a cue.

People with a laughter habit continuously generate thoughts of laughter, positivity, play, and gratitude. We are

---

24 James Clear, *Atomic Habits* (New York: Avery, Imprint of Penguin Random House, LLC, 2018), 55.

plotting, scheming, and wondering *where* and *with whom* we can smile or laugh. Reminders play a key role.

Start with a Plan

> "Our goals can only be reached through a vehicle of a plan, in which we must fervently believe, and upon which we must vigorously act. There is no other route to success."
>
> Pablo Picasso, Artist

To make a habit you need a structured plan—which includes the new desired behavior, a time, and a place. For example: *I will do ten Smile-Ups at 8:20 a.m.* [time] *in my car* [place]. *I will do ten more at 10:45 p.m. while I wind down on the couch.* The time and place become triggers to perform the new habit. Note: Don't get caught up in planning an exact time on the clock. For example, the time could be when I wake up, when I get in the car.

Here's what Plan a Habit looks like:

I Will Do X [the new habit, e.g., Smile-Ups] **at Y time, in Z location.** (PLAN)

Plan Laughter Breaths

Laughter Breaths are another good choice. Remember, to do a Laughter Breath, you inhale deeply and exhale with, *HA-HA-HA-HA-HA!* Pick a few times during the day to add Laughter Breaths. Don't forget to pick a place, too.

I will do Laughter Breaths at 10 a.m. in the car.
... at 4 p.m. at my desk.
... right before dinner at the table.
... on the porch, right after I complete my daily walk.

You can even set an alarm on your phone. You're not adding to your overflowing to-do list. You're adding playtime to your day, and laughter breaks to mundane, repetitive tasks.

Expand Your Skills: Stack a Habit

> "Greatness is a lot of small things done well, stacked up on each other."
> Raymond Anthony Lewis, Jr., NFL Football Player

You already have many activities in your daily routine like rolling out of bed, dressing, and brushing your teeth. You can stack a new habit onto any regular activity:

Before or After I Do X [current activity],
I Will Do Y [new habit] (STACK)

Like this:

- Before I get out of bed every morning, I will do ten Smile-Ups.
- After I'm dressed, I will recite my Laughter Declaration in the mirror.
- After my morning coffee, before I open the mail, I will clap and say, *Very Good, Very Good, YAY!*

An easy way to add several new desired behaviors to your daily routines is to stack as many new habits as you want. For example, wake up and walk into the bathroom [old habit] then add the following:

- Ten Smile-Ups in the mirror.
- Do ten Smile-ups, then stack ten Laughter Breaths.
- On your last exhale, step into the shower and stack the *Laughter Game* titled Shower Yourself with Laughter.

Have fun looking for places to add your favorite *Laughter Games* throughout the day. Add a stack when you:

- Prepare a meal or wash the dishes.
- Grab the leash to walk the dog.
- Wait—for a boss, team members, store clerks, bank tellers.
- Clean the house or the garage—sweep, dust, or scrub grout with a toothbrush.

Start looking for openings to stack *Laughter Games* throughout your day. You'll be surprised at how easy it becomes once you get started.

Laugh on Cue

> "Between stimulus and response there is a space. In that space is our power to choose our response. In our response lies our growth and our freedom."
>
> Viktor Frankl,
> Austrian psychiatrist, Holocaust survivor

Different from a planned laughter activity, a cue is tied to an event or circumstance rather than a time and place. Any unexpected or unwelcome occurrences can become triggers for laughing and smiling. You'll learn to replace annoyance and negative stress with chuckles as your response to each cue fills you with energy or a newfound attitude.

If **X Happens** [something undesirable],
Then **I'll Do Y** [new laughter habit] (CUE)

For example:

- *If* I find myself stuck in traffic, *then* I will do three sets of ten Smile-Ups to help me stay calm and cheerful.
- *If* I left something essential at home and have to return to retrieve it, *then* I will say, *Very Good, Very Good, YAY!* as I notice the giggle gardens along the route home.
- *If* I make a sales pitch and the prospect responds, "No," *then* I will do three rounds of **E**verything's **G**onna **B**e **O**-**K**ay! (EGBOK!), complete with clapping, and get ready for my next presentation.

The *if/then* structure of a cued habit depends upon an external event. Every new day is a gold mine of opportunities to add laughter. We can adopt Og Mandino's mantra—*this too shall pass*—on our way to laughing with life. Over time, cued habits become a powerful tool to combat stress or change your mindset. *If* I'm feeling stressed, *then* I use laughter tools to help me shift my attitude.

Reassure Your Inner Voice

Often when you are stressed you hear that pesky Inner Voice—the one that sabotages you and shows up when you're running late, distracted, overwhelmed, worried, or having a tough day. Tune in closely when you first hear whispering thoughts of self-doubt and inadequacy.

If your own voice has been hijacked, smile with amusement and recognition. You know what the voice intends, but this time, *you're* going to win. Instead of listening as a sponge ready to absorb the negativity, puff up your chest, and with gusto, declare, "How fascinating!"

Disarming the voice with this unexpected response, you can chuckle at yourself and let laughter settle in. This allows you to take control of the situation, giving you back the power that is yours when you let laughter take center stage.

If you feel stress bubbling up and hear inner rumblings of insecurity, *then*, reassure yourself with an enthusiastic round of confidence-building EGBOK! Let EGBOK! become the first card in your laughter habit cue card deck. It's the perfect preamble to whatever other favorite laughter habits you plan and stack.

LAUGHTER BREAK

Pick Your Path

There are many paths you can take as you begin to create laughter habits.

You may want to start solo.

Make an appointment with yourself in the mirror.

Look deeply into your eyes and appreciate your smile.

Gaze until you see a glimmer of your Inner Child.

Clap your hands in front of the mirror, applauding your Inner Child for meeting you there.

Keep clapping and count to one hundred as fast as you can.

Who laughs first?

The clapping may help the adult in you release the giggles.

Breathe deeply as you clap.

The act of clapping your hands together energizes you—and it's caffeine-free!

Feel the energy-igniting playfulness. Listen for joyful laughter sounds.

Without even thinking about it you may have just picked up a new favorite activity.

Congratulate yourself with a final round of applause.

Create Your Alter Ego

Take another look in the mirror. Is there a superpower you'd like to add to your persona so you can become an even better version of your wonderful self? According to *The Alter Ego Effect*, by Todd Herman, you can designate an object to remind you of a hero who most embodies the quality you long to have.[25]

You can do this with anything. To train for a marathon, wear a jersey with the number of your favorite athlete. When you're ready to go for the gold, put on a pair of *Alter Ego* running shoes, or wear a gold medal around your neck as you practice your favorite sport. Want to perfect gourmet baking? Grab a spatula like the one used by a famous French pastry chef.

If you want to become a master laugher, choose an object that reminds you of someone who embodies laughter. It can be someone famous, like your favorite comedian. Or, it can be someone like cousin Peggy on the kiddie train, a person you know who's the life of the party. If we chose Peggy, we'd use a prop to remind us of the way she filled us with laughter at Disneyland: a toy train, a fun hat, or maybe even an exotic bird, whose chortles mimic her incredible laugh.

Creating and reciting a declaration of whatever persona you want to create is a great way to strengthen your developing habits. For Rachael, her declaration is still most effective when recited in front of a mirror.

---

25 Todd Herman, *The Alter Ego Effect: The Power of Secret Identities to Transform Your Life* (New York: Harper Collins Publishers, 2019).

Find a Laughter Buddy

Once you've mastered generating joyful laughter by following the solo path, you may want to expand your reach and invite someone to join you. Rachael was going through an emotionally difficult time and, of course, called Sarah. Sarah said, "Since you're not here to laugh with me in person, go to the mirror. You see me, right? We look alike, so pretend you're seeing me. Do Smile-Ups with me in the mirror. Now let's laugh."

Realizing this was effective even on the phone, Sarah called Rachael proactively a few times to elevate her mood. Within minutes of Sarah's encouraging laughter, Rachael consistently felt uplifted and energized.

Sarah decided to establish a weekly Laughter Club on the phone. Dr. Kataria asks all certified Laughter Yoga leaders to offer a regular Laughter Club. The idea is to make laughter as widely accessible as possible. Generally, Laughter Clubs are free opportunities for people to gather in groups to share laughter, face to face, on the phone, or virtually, with a certified leader. Sarah's Laughter Club has been on Monday mornings ever since. Hundreds of people from around the world have joined her on the phone for more than a decade. All are welcome. (See our website.)

The phone format works perfectly for those who prefer to laugh with others and are unable to attend a local Laughter Club in person. It's also a safe place to begin a regular laughter habit. Sarah didn't set out to create a powerful laughter habit for herself. However, as the years went on, she realized that's exactly what she had done. Now, every Monday, Sarah and dozens of her followers set their alarms for 9:00 a.m. They've made it a practice, a life-long habit, to connect and laugh together on the phone every week.

Make a Difference with Laughter

Sometimes in life it's easier to provide something for someone else. In the process, you may be surprised to find unintended personal benefits. When Rachael tried to coax herself into laughing every day, she found distractions and waning commitment. By undertaking to laugh on camera every day for forty days and promising to share a daily photo or video of herself on social media, Rachael had put herself in the hot seat. By the third day of posting a video of herself laughing, her confidence began to grow. After a week, a friend responded to one of the posts and asked if an accountability partner was available. Rachael jumped right into the role. Emboldened by the need to show up for someone else, Rachael redoubled her resolve. Rachael credits the friend's request for a partner with the successful completion of her first 40-Day Laughter Challenge.

Holding someone accountable for a promise they make may have you show up for the other person while serving as a reminder of your own commitments. Starting any new habit—a new diet, exercise plan, or adding more laughter to your day—may be more fun and more successful with a buddy. You can be the one to bring laughter into your workplace, gym, school, or ... *anywhere*. Notice, you're learning not just to laugh on cue, but to become that cue for others.

Have at Least One of Your Several Laughter Buddies on Speed Dial

We're all prone to forget about laughter sometimes. Laughter Buddies help remind us that laughter is readily available as a wonderful response to stress and disappointment. As a child, you instinctively knew you'd have more fun with a playmate—even an imaginary one. When you have a Laughter Buddy on speed dial, life is more fun. Lean on your buddy, and you'll be surrounded by laughter. Your joyful energy may even attract new friends. The truth is, we're always attracting *something*. Why not be a magnet for joy?

Aristotle said, "We are what we repeatedly do. Excellence, then, is not an act, but a habit." Laughter habits include responding to life with laughter and reaching out to a buddy for support when you're seeking more fun and connection. Remember, laughter habits are not mastered all at once. Fill your days with buckets of giggles, chuckles, and chortles, and build a list of buddies you can call upon.

We've taught you what a laughter habit is and given you the formulas so you can easily create your own. Play with the ideas in this chapter to ignite your creativity. How wonderful it would be if we could become our own first responders when faced with a problem or hardship.

By creating laughter habits, we hope laughter will become so second nature it will dispel stress, pain, and overwhelm. Expand your toolkit and keep it handy. You don't have to have troubles to enjoy a laugh. We like to think that's why Charlie Chaplain said, "A day without laughter is a day wasted."

"Each of us has a spark of life inside us, and our highest endeavor ought to be to set off that spark in one another."

Kenny Ausubel, Filmmaker

Ten

Connect and Celebrate with Laughter

Laughter and joy are elemental to being human. When we appreciate the need for connection, we can fully embrace what laughter offers—a golden opportunity to deepen our relationships. Robert Provine, the world's leading scientific expert on laughter, conducted his own research and proved that laughter is contagious. He found it serves as a powerful nonverbal communication tool. Further, he discovered, through extensive observation, that people are thirty times more likely to laugh in social settings while interacting with others than they are to laugh alone.[26] Shared laughter enhances and improves human interactions of all kinds. From turning strangers into friends, to rebuilding broken love relationships, laughing together can strengthen the foundation of even your most challenging encounters with others.

---

26 Robert R. Provine, *Laughter: A Scientific Investigation* (New York: Penguin Books, 2000), 43-48.

While we laugh naturally as infants, we learn early in life that laughter is a vital social skill. According to Professor Sophie Scott, Deputy Director of the Institute for Cognitive Neuroscience at University College London, laughter is an important social skill worth consciously developing. This skill involves learning how to engage in any circumstance with laughter. Scott has noticed in her research that when everyone is included, laughter has the power to enhance the positive mood of a group of people.[27]

It is easy to laugh at a comedy club, or when your uncle makes a joke, and harder to laugh when tough stuff happens. It is equally important to be able to consciously lighten the mood or generate intimacy with another person when involved in a serious or emotionally sensitive conversation. According to comedian, Victor Borge, "Laughter is the shortest distance between two people."

Rachael

Laughter and Intimacy

Enda Junkins is one of America's leading experts on Laughter Therapy and a practicing psychotherapist. In her book, *Belly Laughter in Relationships: Something Else Positive Below the Belt*, Junkins said that her first marriage suffered and ended partly

---

[27] Sophie Scott, "Why We Should Take Laughter More Seriously," TEDxExeter, June 7, 2018, 13:03, https://www.youtube.com/watch?v=TKYwGYrVm0o.

because she and her ex-husband stopped laughing together. She seemed to be speaking directly to me. My husband and I don't spend a lot of time laughing. He is a fountain of quips and jokes, but we just don't have the same sense of humor.

After reading Junkins' book and contemplating our predictable future measured by the frequency of our shared laughter, I concluded: *if I want more positivity in my marriage, I'll have to find my own way to initiate more laughter.* I decided to test one of Junkins' laughter tools on the spot. I walked into my husband's office, took his hands in mine, looked into his eyes, and playfully insisted, "Laugh with me." Caught off-guard, he chuckled a little. As I laughed out loud, he humored me, and we shared a genuine moment of connection. I patted myself on the back. I wasn't asking for anything: no complaints, no problems to solve, nothing special to tell him. In creating a bit of tenderness, we got closer. In my ongoing quest to add more laughter to my life, I'm gradually becoming more light-hearted. I've created affectionate laughter memories with my husband. He joins me in occasional laughter interruptions that leave us both with a smile and fresh endorphins. It is not a panacea, but it is has become a valuable tool.

While writing this portion of the book, I asked my husband if he felt more connected or closer after these random sixty-second laughter encounters that I initiate. He confessed that he doesn't feel any increased closeness or connection, but he's always happy to accept my requests, especially knowing it helps me.

I feel more connected because the playfulness helps me show up in a more lighthearted way.

Laughing adds fun and connection to our relationship. ～

LAUGHTER GAME

Hold Hands and Laugh

Open yourself up to sharing playful laughter with significant people in your life.

1. Hold hands with your partner.
2. Take a deep breath as you tune in to each other and synchronize your breathing.
3. Look into each other's eyes and laugh together.

The contagious nature of laughter transforms a serious mood into a playful possibility.

Do you feel differently toward each other? Did you notice your mood elevate?

In relationships, Junkins asserts that laughter builds trust and establishes intimacy and bonding. Loss of laughter can cause a relationship to become brittle and break. Can you imagine inviting strangers to laugh with you? Enlivened by her success with her husband, Rachael began engaging playfully with strangers. Once, she entered an elevator in a court house and surprised herself when she blurted out, "Quick, everybody, laugh out loud with me!" Then she burst out laughing! She smiled for the rest of the day imagining the folks on the elevator retelling the story. They may not have laughed with Rachael in the moment, but odds are they caught the giggles afterward. Rachael has incorporated Sophie Scott's message, to take laughter seriously, into her life: "Think about your laughter. Don't undervalue or trivialize your laughter. It matters. It matters a lot. It can sound like friendship. It can sometimes sound a lot like love."[28]

Celebrate Life with Laughter

Holidays and rituals have the unique feature of bringing people together to engage in joyful celebration. A perfect example of a ceremony that brings people together for the purpose of laughter is the Navajo tradition that welcomes a new baby into the family at the time of the baby's first laugh. This first laugh signifies the child's readiness to fully transition from the spirit world into the physical world. Family and

---

28 Sophie Scott, "Why We Should Take Laughter More Seriously," TEDxExeter, June 7, 2018, 13:03,
   https://www.youtube.com/watch?v=TKYwGYrVm0o.

friends eagerly compete to see who will earn the baby's first laugh. That person is honored as the organizer of The First Laugh Ceremony, A'wee Chi'deedloh. The baby is viewed as the host of the party and distributes a bag of goodies to each guest in the spirit of generosity, a prized virtue and value of the Navajo.[29] What a profound way to honor laughter and acknowledge the presence of laughter in the baby's life by the entire community.

In Japan, a Shinto shrine is the site of the Waraiko Ceremony in which farmers offer their heartiest laughter as a gift to the gods. This laughing ritual originated in the 1200s and continues today. On the first Sunday in December, teams of two sit facing each other and offer three distinct guffaws: one to show gratitude for the year's harvest, one to pray for a good harvest the following year, and a third to laugh all of their troubles away. Overseen by the Chief Priest of the Shinto shrine, the teams are judged on whether their laughs are in sync with one another, and whether their laughs are sincere or too timid. Both team members laugh from the bottom of their hearts until they are able to laugh in perfect unison. The Chief Priest bangs on a metal tub to indicate success or failure for each team. The same metal tub has been used for the last 50 years.[30]

---

29   Ingrid Fetell Lee, "The Navajo Celebration of a Baby's First Laugh," *The Aesthetics of Joy,* https://aestheticsofjoy.com/navajo-celebration-babys-first-laugh/.

30   Ministry of Foreign Affairs of Japan, Web Japan, Kids Web Japan, "Waraiko (Laughing Your Way to Heaven)." https://web-japan.org/kidsweb/explore/calendar/december/waraiko.html.

Perhaps the best example of incorporating laughter as a way of life is expressed by the Chinese fable of the Three Laughing Monks. Cherished and esteemed as unique spiritual mentors, the monks demonstrated how to embrace life as a grand opportunity for laughter. As the legend goes, three monks traveled from town to town, across China, merely laughing—without speaking. They stood in the center of each town they visited and laughed with their whole bodies, minds, and hearts. Crowds gathered to watch and listen as their prayers, expressed by contagious laughter, spread throughout the town.

One day, after many years of traveling together sharing laughter, one of the monks died. Expecting grief and tears, the village people gathered with curiosity. They were surprised to find the two remaining monks laughed harder than ever. One of the villagers approached and asked, "How can you laugh at a time like this?"

For the first time, the monks spoke. They said, "Because yesterday, on our way to your village, our friend proposed a bet on who of us would beat the other two and die first. And now he won, the old rogue! He even had a testament prepared!"

According to tradition, dead bodies must be washed and their clothing changed before being put on the funeral pyre. The dead monk had urged his friends, "Don't give me a bath because I have never been unclean. So much laughter has been in my life that no impurity can accumulate or come to me. I have not gathered any dust. Laughter is always young and fresh."

To respect his wishes, the dead monk's clothes were not changed. While putting the monk's body on the fire, his friends noticed some Chinese fireworks hidden under his clothes. As the fireworks started to go off, the villagers began to laugh. The two remaining monks noted that even in death, their friend had managed to win—he got the last laugh.

The monks committed their lives to being an example of confronting challenges with a light-hearted spirit, showing how laughter possesses the power to dissolve any adversity. They reminded the villagers their very own joy is what breathes life into their beings.

SPEED BUMP

Are You a Laughing Monk?

LAUGHTER PARTICIPATION SCALE

- Uninhibited and Free
- Eager
- Engaged
- Willing to Experiment
- Curious
- Cautious
- Skeptical
- Fearful
- Not Interested at All

How does this legend of the Three Laughing Monks inform your thinking about laughter and its place in your life?

Can you see yourself embracing a life of laughter as easily as the monks did?

Could you try it for a day or even an hour?

Good thing we're only suggesting fifteen minutes!

Take note of where you are on the *Laughter Participation Scale* and use the rest of this chapter to help you move up.

Laughter Holidays to Tickle Your Funny Bone

World Laughter Day (WLD)

When you think about holidays you likely conjure pictures of family and friends gathering as you recall sounds of shared laughter. It's almost as if laughter is the life of the party, adding memories and fun. The Navajo aren't the only ones to center a holiday around laughter. Dr. Madan Kataria created the first mega-laughter party with 12,000 Laughter Club members in 1998 in Mumbai, India, calling it World Laughter Day. Kataria used this party to raise awareness of the healing benefits of laughter and to promote world peace. Since then, on the first Sunday in May of every year, thousands of Laughter Club members host World Laughter Day celebrations at major parks and landmarks all over the world.

Like all those being trained, Sarah learned of this holiday when she became a Laughter Yoga leader. After Sarah was certified to train other Laughter Yoga leaders, she made it a point to take her students to a public place to practice engaging strangers in laughter. Once, on World Laughter Day, armed with an assortment of colorful hats and posters, they headed to a public park, searching for playgrounds. Sarah instinctively knew kids would be eager to join in the merriment. With enthusiasm and all the playfulness they could muster, Sarah and her students invited the kids to choose a hat and celebrate World Laughter Day as they belted out their best laughs together. Photos with the colorful posters and silly poses captured the spirit of the day. Parents looked on with curiosity, but soon the kids were asking their parents to don a hat and join the fun. It wasn't long before Sarah and her students had everyone in a circle as they led a laughter session. A good time was had by all.

Rachael happened to be part of this experience at the park. Recognizing that not all the onlookers were willing to participate, she had an idea. We created a permission slip for hesitant adults, to provide them permission to play, have fun, and celebrate all opportunities for laughter. In subsequent celebrations, we've noticed an increase in participation when we hand out the permission slips. The colorful hats and posters help—we're happy to receive lots of giggles and more willing participation from both the kids and the adults.

PERMISSION TO PLAY

To: Me
From: Me
Re: **Have Fun & Seize the Moment**

With a smile, I hereby grant myself full access to my Inner Child. I have unlimited permission to:

**have fun ~ play full-out
act silly ~ laugh freely**

BONUS:
Exponential joy when shared with friends and strangers.

Fully transferable   Redeem anytime   Unlimited uses
Expiration Date: Never

Global Belly Laugh Day (GBLD)

Sarah continued seeking laughter holidays and was elated to discover the existence of another international holiday called Global Belly Laugh Day, created in 2006 by Elaine Helle, to remind people of the great gifts of smiles and laughter, and to infuse the day with play. Elaine encourages people to participate in the Great Belly Laugh Bounce Around the World on January 24th at exactly 1:24 p.m. local time, wherever they find themselves. For Sarah, it became the perfect motivation to practice belly laughing throughout the year. Her *Laughter Game* of choice is Gradient Laughter.

LAUGHTER GAME

Gradient Laughter

1. Sit or squat down, curling yourself in a ball as much as possible as you begin to giggle softly.
2. As you slowly sit upright or stand, gradually turn up the volume of your laughter—adding chuckles, cackles, and snorts.
3. Laugh louder and deeper as you throw your head back and raise your arms in the air.
4. Breathe again and laugh the BIGGEST belly laugh you possibly can.
5. When you've laughed so hard you feel like a deflated balloon, turn down the volume on your laughter until it's a quiet giggle as you return to a sitting/squatting position.
6. Take a deep breath. Repeat until you become comfortable, building to stronger and more vibrant laughter each time.

Sarah found it easy and fun to promote and engage with Global Belly Laugh Day. She infused Gradient Laughter into many laughter sessions and used the game as a way to both practice deep belly laughs and to prepare for the holiday, even months ahead of time.

International Moment of Laughter Day (IMOLD)

Global Belly Laugh Day helped beat the Minnesota winter blues with laughter. By February Sarah was on the lookout for more fun holidays. She discovered humorologist Izzy Gessel's holiday, International Moment of Laughter Day (IMOLD), marking April 14th as a day to remind people to laugh out loud *every* day. Izzy believes laughing comes right after breathing as the healthiest thing you can do for yourself. The motivation for IMOLD was to encourage people to find and focus on the positive by inserting moments of smiles and laughter throughout the day. He specifically chose a day when many Americans find themselves feeling stressed, the day before Tax Day in the United States, because he knows laughter helps us de-stress.

As Sarah contemplated the ironic proximity of IMOLD to the infamously stressful April 15th tax deadline, she had an idea. She called her accountant and volunteered to lead his entire office in a free half-hour Laughter Yoga session on April 14th. He enthusiastically accepted, and she provided a much-appreciated laughter break. At the end of the session he asked, "How much do I owe you?" She reiterated her intention to show gratitude by gifting the laughter session. To her delightful surprise he insisted on paying her. She laughed all the way to the bank!

Pausing to celebrate IMOLD inspires people to take time to smell the roses, stop fretting, and laugh with others. One of the activities Izzy suggests, aimed at adding laughter to the day, is collecting jokes and sharing them like Madan Kataria once did.

Sarah has a hard time remembering jokes, even the ones she finds funny. She often fantasized that she'd be able to hold people's attention while reciting a brilliant joke. She imagined hearing a flourish of infectious laughter as she confidently took a bow.

Despite trying to commit a few of her favorite jokes to memory and practicing her delivery, she was never able to accomplish this to her satisfaction.

Sarah knows it's not necessary to be a masterful comedian with perfect timing and delivery to create laughter—she often stimulates intentional joyous laughter. For people who secretly wish to be distinguished joke-tellers, Sarah figured out a way to end their struggle and find success. She wrote a book called *Jokes By Number*.

Spoiler alert: the best joke book of all time contains no words. Instead, the book is filled with a selection of numbers, each representing a different hilarious joke.

LAUGHTER GAME

Jokes by Number

In this *Laughter Game*, we figuratively join the joke-telling experts of the world at a joke-telling conference. Armed with a copy of Sarah's book, *Jokes by Number*, we imagine ourselves gathering to practice our delivery. As each joke-teller calls out a favorite number, we respond with side-splitting, knee-slapping, uproarious laughter as we applaud one another.

1. Open the book and scan until you find the number of your favorite joke.
2. Be sure to proclaim the number with enthusiasm and panache.
3. The crowd follows your lead and erupts with roll-on-the-floor, infectious laughter!
4. Pass the book to the next person and repeat.

Let laughter holidays tickle your funny bone. Laughter leaders around the world host parties in person and online to celebrate these annual laughter holidays. Invite a friend to join you as you connect with fellow laughers and celebrate laughter together.

Add Laughter to Your Favorite Traditional Holiday

When laughter steps out from the spotlight and is no longer the main theme or focus of a holiday, it still waits in the wings, ready to step forward in an instant at any party or holiday gathering. You can pump up your energy and get into the mood for any party with a playlist of upbeat tunes and laughter songs. "Happy" by Pharrell Williams will likely get you and your guests dancing and singing. "I Love to Laugh" from *Mary Poppins* can set the perfect tone for laughing.

Why not choose smiles and laughter as the decor for your next party? You can easily find smile and laughter emoji plates, napkins, and centerpieces to brighten the space and get everyone giggling as they arrive—or design your own decorations. Offer a selection of laughter-themed food: Snickers, Almond Joy, Laughing Cow Cheese, and Laughy Taffy. You can add a smiling face to a pizza or put ketchup and mustard smiling faces on burgers. Have fun sleuthing for other smile and laughter-themed ideas to set a practically perfect positively perky party atmosphere.

Need fresh ideas for a party activity? Mix up the seating to encourage new connections. Have two sets of place cards with laughter sounds printed on them. As people arrive, have them choose a card they like. Once they find the matching card on the table, they take their seat. Invite them to make the sound on the card they chose. At a graduation party, deliver a speech, *Laughter Advice for the Graduate.* You'll be prepared with all your newly acquired information and skills from this book! Invite others to contribute their own advice.

Gifts are an added bonus to any milestone. Grab a giggle from your pocket and put a smile on your face. These are the gifts that truly keep on giving, benefiting both giver and receiver. We hope these ideas will help rouse your party-planning excitement.

It's easy to connect with laughter while celebrating a laughter holiday. We hope you'll begin to add play and creativity to every day of the year. We uncovered scores of interesting fun holidays to add mirth and a new twist to ordinary days. We found monthly themes to stimulate your creativity and included them in the calendar below as well. For instance, June is *Rebuild Your Life Month.* You can start the month with a new project at home or at work, some new habits, or changes to your daily schedule. Be on the lookout for adding spurts of laughter to each change you make. Stack a new habit every day as you rebuild your life, and be sure some of the new stacks include chuckles, guffaws, and plenty of play. Do this throughout the month and you'll surely be ready for *National Day of Joy* on June 28th. Post this *Fun Holidays Calendar* on your refrigerator. Let it capture your attention and trigger laughter as you imagine what you will celebrate next.

FUN HOLIDAYS CALENDAR

Monthly	Theme	Holiday	Date
Jan	Be On Purpose Month	Global Belly Laugh Day	Jan 24
Feb	National Laugh Friendly Month	Laugh & Get Rich Day	Feb 8
Mar	Women's History Month	Let's Laugh Day	Mar 19
Apr	National Stress Awareness Month	Int'l Moment of Laughter Day	Apr 14
May	Mental Health Awareness Month	World Laughter Day	1st Sunday
Jun	Rebuild Your Life Month	National Day of Joy	Jun 28
Jul	Good Care Month	International Self-Care Day	Jul 24
Aug	Family Fun Month	Book Lover's Day	Aug 9
Sep	Friendship Month	Positive Thinking Day	Sep 13
Oct	Bullying Prevention Month	World Smile Day	1st Friday
Nov	Family Care-Givers' Month	World Kindness Day	Nov 13
Dec	Read A New Book Month	Make Up Your Mind [to Laugh] Day	Dec 31

Use Laughter to Celebrate Daily Wins

You don't have to wait for holidays to surround yourself with Laughter Buddies. Be on a constant lookout for places to add laughter. You can incorporate a mini-laughter celebration into your daily wins—big or small. We encourage you to insert intentional laughter to elevate ordinary events, too. Let's use the laughter cue formula to help you.

When A Happens [ordinary thing],
Then I'll Do B [add smiles and laughter]. (CUE)

- *When* I succeed in parallel parking in an extremely tight space, *then* I will laugh out loud and clap with glee at my good fortune in finding a space and applaud my parking skills with a *Very Good, Very Good, Yippee!*
- *When* I'm working on being on time, and I arrive with a minute to spare, *then,* I will take a deep breath, exhale with a sigh of contentment, and keep a smile plastered on my face.
- *When* I look out the window to check the weather, *then* I will respond with a different laughter sound based on what I see and what I have planned for the day. For example, clouds may elicit a giggle since I planned to read a good book. Rain may cause a roar since I had a picnic planned. Sunshine will trigger a belly

laugh as I pack up for the beach. Snow will bring forth a snort as I prepare to shovel the walk. Colorful fall leaves with a gentle wind will leave me chuckling with fond childhood memories of chasing falling leaves.

Go ahead, celebrate life with joyous laughter. Instead of bemoaning the rain, seize the opportunity to jump in mud puddles. Open your eyes to find free associations of gratitude and stimulate chuckles of celebration and joy, no matter what the weather.

Why do this? So you can energize and memorialize the moments of your life. Never give up on the child inside you. Make a habit of acknowledging yourself and others in a positive, congratulatory way. Champion your successes with laughter.

Rachael

Honor People with Laughter, Too

Let's not stop at celebrating life's little moments. Let's create mini-gratitude/acknowledgment parties to recognize the many unsung heroes and heroines in our lives. Hearts, flowers, and chocolate are routine. Let's spice it up with a mini-laughter celebration to say thanks.

Please join me now as I publicly acknowledge Sarah for all she's taught me through the years. Grandpa Barney got it right when she was born, *"Very Good, Very Good, YIPPEE!"* You can imagine the bouquets of flowers, the huge heart-shaped box of chocolate, and the long loving hug as I thank Sarah for helping me laugh more easily. Of course, I will engage her in a full fifteen minutes of joyous belly laughter to crown her achievements. She wasn't just our mother's *Bonus Baby*. Really, she was *mine!* ~

"Isn't it astonishing that all these secrets have been preserved for so many years just so we could discover them!"

The Wright Brothers,
Aviation Pioneers

Eleven

Laughter Discoveries: Past, Present, Future

For us, reading about laughter has become as contagious as a full-blown belly laugh. Once we started reading, we couldn't stop being excited about the next treasure we'd uncover. So much of the information we found inspired us. We hope our discoveries below will spark your interest so you can experience some of the same *ah-ha* moments we did.

Not-So-Funny Moments in the History of Laughter

Why are we including anything negative about laughter when our goal is to uplift you?

It's not just the fact that there *were* negative views of laughter, but imagine *your* life without laughter. What would that even look like? Throughout history, the impact of these negative views played out in rather extreme ways. Even as we point these out, we are overcome with gratitude that we do not live in a world void of play and laughter.

Sarah was once reprimanded for laughing at the back of a classroom, but that's nothing compared to what happened when you got caught laughing in the 1100's. The common view was that neither speechmaker nor kings should laugh, and one must never mock a monarch. A subject in King Henry I of England's court dared to speak the truth to the monarch, and mocked him in jest. Consequently, the King ordered the man's eyes to be gouged out.

In the 1600s, the Puritans viewed laughter as sinful, ungodly, corrupt, and intolerable. Christians were encouraged to live serious lives. By the mid-1600s, when the Puritans ruled England, comedies were outlawed.

Even in the 1700s, when attitudes toward mirth had begun to shift, there were still concerns about engaging in laughter. Imagine if Lord Chesterfield, Phillip Dormer Stanhope, 4th Earl of Chesterfield, British statesman, diplomat, and man of letters were *your* father. He is best known for writing *Letters to His Son on the Art of Becoming a Man of the World and a Gentleman,* published after his death, in 1774. Here are some excerpts from his letters:

> "A gentleman may smile, but he never laughs aloud in company; for the laugh of a gentleman is too serious a thing to be wasted on trifles, and too valuable to be thrown away in public."
>
> "Having mentioned laughing, I must particularly warn you against it: and I could heartily wish, that you may often be seen to smile, but *never* heard to laugh while you live." [Emphasis ours]

"In my mind, there is nothing so illiberal, and so ill-bred, as audible laughter."[31]

Really, Dad . . . this is the legacy you want to leave me . . . ? Can't you picture Chesterfield's poor son on any occasion when he had the misfortune of laughing out loud and the guilt he must have felt?

In 1875, George Vasey wrote *The Philosophy of Laughter and Smiling*, a classic in the anti-laughter genre. *Wait—there's such a thing as an anti-laughter genre of books? Yep. It's a thing. You might have trouble finding it; we stumbled upon it by accident.* According to John Morreall in his book, *Humor Works*, the English poet Shelley was a prominent anti-laughter spokesman. Morreall quotes Shelley who wrote in the early 1800s, "I am convinced there can be no entire regeneration of mankind until laughter is put down."[32]

Vasey believed laughter was both physically and morally dangerous, a symptom of modern civilization, commercialized by humorists who spread the unnatural behavior. He called for the complete elimination of laughter in favor of smiling. Vasey believed laughter was freakish. He vividly described what happened to a person when they laughed, including distortions of the body, convulsions, disagreeable vulgar sounds, and the inability to engage in thinking, speaking, or acting in any voluntary way. He contrasted this sharply

---

31 Philip Dormer Stanhope, 4th Earl of Chesterfield, *Letters to His Son on the Fine Art of Becoming a Man of the World and a Gentleman* (London: 1774).

32 John Morreall, PhD, *Humor Works* (Massachusetts: HRD Press, 1997), 3.

with the smile of sincerity, candor, and benevolence, in which "the thoughts are the purest, the words are the gentlest, and the actions are the kindest!"[33] Vasey perceived "that laughter does not make a good man, and that there are thousands of good men who never laugh."[34] His book includes drawings of people laughing to demonstrate the most extreme distortions to make his point.

We're sure glad we never met Mr. Vasey. We can't imagine he was a very joyful fellow.

Searching for Why People Laugh

Have you ever stopped to wonder *why* people laugh? Our father was a high school civics teacher and offered weekly seminars for his students at our home. What young kid doesn't feel important being around a bunch of high school seniors? Of all the seminars over the years, Sarah recalls only one topic: *What makes people laugh?* She has no memory of what was said that night, but it did spark her curiosity. She never imagined she would one day be able to provide educated answers to that question. Rachael doesn't recall this specific seminar at all, but is eager to field questions about laughter after all her research.

---

33 George Vasey, *The Philosophy of Laughter and Smiling*, (London: J. Burns, 1875), 125.

34 Vasey, *Philosophy of Laughter and Smiling*, 125.

Laughter—A Powerful Field of Study

The familiar adage, "Laughter is the best medicine" has been around for a very long time, though no one seems to know its exact origins. Early laughter histories paint laughter, humor, and comedy as predominantly negative. More recently, however, the positive effects of laughter are being recognized across multiple disciplines. In fact, laughter is now viewed as a powerful field of study in its own right.

Some people may recognize Gelatology as the name of a local ice cream shop in Las Vegas. For laughter enthusiasts, however, *gelotology* is laughter's very own field of study. The term was coined in 1964 by William F. Fry, professor of psychology at Stanford University Medical School in California, an expert on health and laughter. Fry was motivated by the verse in Proverbs that compares joyfulness to good medicine. As the first *gelotologist*, he was also the first to apply for and secure public funding for laughter research to study the psychological and physiological effects of humor on the body.

How did laughter gain credibility? We had no idea how far back in time we would travel as we began to explore laughter, and we were surprised to find it in so many diverse areas of study. We found ourselves delving into the subjects of religion, philosophy, psychology, physiology, medicine, neuroscience, integrative medicine, humor, comedy, theater, literature, and others.

No discussion of laughter would be complete without considering the different theories purported throughout the ages to explain laughter. Though literally one hundred different theories of laughter have been catalogued, fear not, we are only discussing our top five.

Theories to Explain the Usefulness of Laughter

Even this very brief look at the main theories of laughter will help you understand some of the vacillating views of laughter over time. Philosophers and scientists love studying different topics and labelling them. We are more concerned with spreading healthy laughter. The theories we've chosen to summarize provide a historical context that helps us understand many nuances of the entire practice of laughter.

Superiority Theory

The Superiority Theory can best be understood as laughing at the misfortune of others. There is a common human tendency to look down triumphantly on someone else. The laughter expresses ridicule, mockery, and scorn. This theory had a strong influence in the church and in politics.

We were both drawn to Laughter Yoga because it rejects making fun of anyone. By creating a safe space with agreements from all participants to bring acceptance rather than judgment, the possibility of ridicule or mockery is removed.

Incongruity Theory

Often a speaker or comedian sets up an expectation and then gets a laugh by ending the story with a surprise ending. This is just one example of the incongruity theory in which laughter is triggered as a way to resolve the cognitive dissonance. In life, when we are surprised by something unanticipated, we often laugh as a way to overcome awkwardness and restore balance.

Relief/Repression Theory

The Relief/Repression Theory suggests that laughter provides comfort and relief and serves as a cathartic experience which helps alleviate stress, tension, and anxiety. In *Philosophy of Humor*, philosopher John Morreall describes the Relief Theory as "an hydraulic explanation in which laughter does in the nervous system what a pressure-relief valve does in a steam boiler."[35] He credits Lord Shaftesbury with sketching this pressure-relief valve in his 1709 essay, *An Essay on the Freedom of Wit and Humor*. Morreall suggested that early laughter may have been an indication of shared relief after danger passed. The fight-or-flight response to a threat is inhibited by the relaxation that comes at the end of laughter.

The Release of Energy Theory

Similar to the Relief/Repression Theory, the Release of Energy Theory focuses more on the physical aspects of laughter as a way to release energy. Both a physical and emotional release occur via increased heart rate, deep breathing, and muscles engaged during laughter.

---

35   John Morreall, PhD, "Philosophy of Humor," *The Stanford Encyclopedia of Philosophy* (Summer 2023 Edition), Edward N. Zalta & Uri Nodelman (eds.). https://plato.stanford.edu/entries/humor/.

The Play Theory

Laughter and smiles were early play signals that communicated no real danger was present. Play trains us for the unexpected as we simulate risk and learn to recover. The Play Theory emphasizes the intrinsic joy and pleasure derived from playful activities, and laughter is seen as an expression of that joy. The Play Theory connects laughter to playfulness, overall well-being, and the social benefits of shared laughter.

These theories originated far back in time, as long ago as when the ancient Greek philosopher Socrates lived. As we read, we often felt like Alice in Wonderland, wondering what rabbit hole we had fallen into. The names of people who had something to say about laughter read like a historical Who's Who. We decided to do a little name-dropping, as we spent so much time poring over their ideas they started to feel like our personal mentors. You might not immediately associate these historical figures with laughter, and yet, here they are popping up in the midst of our laughter explorations: Plato, Aristotle, René Descartes, Sigmund Freud, Immanuel Kant, Martin Luther, Voltaire, Henri Bergson, John Dewey, Søren Kierkegaard, and Thomas Aquinas. Imagine the dinner conversation you could have with this group.

You may want to do your own research based on your particular interests. It's like putting together a giant puzzle without knowing ahead of time what the finished picture will look like. To include all the fascinating figures and information they contributed to the laughter conversation is fodder for another book, but we couldn't help whetting your appetite.

Do All Roads Lead to Playful Laughter?

When King Henry II took the throne in England (1154-1189), there was chaos and anarchy. He introduced innovative governmental policies and procedural reforms in an attempt to restore order and regulate political life. He began to use laughter as an effective political tool. His courtiers increasingly spoke about the value of laughter to help them get things done. Rivals could be brought down with a well-timed joke. Corruption could be exposed using satire. Enemies could be undermined with strategic laughter. Making others laugh was viewed as honorable—a huge shift from earlier views casting laughter as damnable behavior.

While we don't want to go on record as sanctioning laughter as a tool for manipulation, we are encouraged to see laughter being viewed more positively.

Laughter became a powerful way to relieve tremendous tensions. Under Henry II, people close to him could employ laughter as a way to communicate satiric messages or criticisms and the King would listen, though perhaps not agree. A far cry from his grandfather's gouging out eyes, he had learned to use laughter as a powerful tool to maintain and negotiate power.[36]

Throughout the Middle Ages (500 CE - 1450s) court jesters played a much more significant role in the court than

---

36 Peter Jones, *Serious Science,* "History of Laughter" (March 24, 2020). https://serious-science.org/history-of-laughter-9786.

merely to entertain. Also known as truth tellers, they were found in royal courts throughout medieval and Renaissance Europe. From Beatrice K. Otto's book, *Fools are Everywhere: The Court Jester Around the World,* we learned that jesters permeated China, India, Japan, Russia, and even America and Africa. While the presence of royal jesters died out after a relatively short period of time, domestic jesters became common around the world.

We were surprised to learn that during the Renaissance, jesters tended to be disabled, dwarves, hunchbacks, or societal outcasts. Even so, they were often admired for their quick wit. Many enjoyed a seat at the table and were permitted to speak their thoughts freely without fear of retribution. By the late Middle Ages the jester was granted "comic dispensation," permitted to give his master an honest assessment of his actions, decisions, and even his character. These nearly universal court "fools" were specifically selected to entertain, advise, and even to help the king take a real look at himself. Our book, too, uses laughter as a tool to help you get to know yourself better. No roasting required.

Laughter— A Long-Standing Remedy

Imagine yourself living in a different time. Whatever ails you, you seek a remedy. Let's explore the historical journey that led us to the awareness of laughter's many physical benefits. Don't worry, there will be no quiz at the end, in case the mention of a historical journey triggered you. We are eager to share what we found most fascinating in order to create a context for the ever-changing views of laughter.

Early on, the ancient Greeks believed people got sick as a divine punishment and recovered as a merciful gift from the gods. Over time, the physical cause and effect of illnesses began to replace the spiritual beliefs of disease as punishments. In the 1100s, both medical and theological beliefs about laughter began to change. As doctors learned more about the physical body through direct observation, a noticeable shift from the negative toward the positive took root.

Not long after that, laughter was recognized as a powerful healing force within the body by doctors in Salerno, Italy and at Montpellier Medical School in France, the oldest still-active medical school in Europe. By the late 1100s, laughter was seen as a measure of good blood, a good balance of body fluids, and an encouraging sign of good health.

During the 1300s, when humor was being used to distract patients from pain, French surgeon, Henri de Mondeville, taught his students to encourage relatives and friends to cheer recovering patients with jokes and laughter to facilitate their return to health.

By the mid-1500s, an Italian physician, philosopher, and historian, Girolamo Mercuriale, best known for his work on physical exercise and sports medicine, recommended laughter as a form of exercise for the diaphragm and lungs. He believed laughter was good for the body and the mind.

Not only physicians, but an English educator in the 1600s, Richard Mulcaster, headmaster of a school in London, recommended laughter to those suffering from head colds. English physician, Thomas Sydenham, sometimes referred to as the father of English medicine, recommended laughter to treat hysteria and hypochondria.

Richard Mead, physician to the British royal family in the 1700s, helped develop public health policies in England. He recognized the health benefits of laughter and suggested it as a way of reducing stress and anxiety. He believed in the importance of a healthy mind and body and saw laughter as a way to promote overall well-being and health, in addition to its ability to improve social connections, strengthen relationships, and promote joy and goodwill. We wonder what health policies he would create for us today to cope with the levels of stress and anxiety that the information age has brought.

Medical Clowns Bring Laughter to Sick People

In the 1930s, clowns were brought into Unites States' hospitals to cheer up patients recovering from polio. Then, in the 1970s, Hunter Doherty Adams, more commonly known as Patch Adams, an American physician, comedian, social activist, clown, and author, founded the Gesundheit! Institute, a model of holistic medical care that sees the patient as part of a family, community, society, and the world. He trained clowns to use humor and laughter to improve the emotional and physical well-being of the patients and was the catalyst for the creation of thousands of therapeutic care clowns worldwide.

Training programs for medical clowning in hospitals sprang up in the late 1970s and 1980s, including the Big Apple Circus training program in New York City.

In 2002, Yaacov Shriqui, founded the non-profit, *The Dream Doctors,* in Israel. They integrate professional medical clowns into Israeli hospitals by training them to work as members of multidisciplinary care teams. The clowns operate as paraprofessionals and are committed to improving patient well-being and enhancing the efficacy of healthcare delivery. *The Dream Doctors* also train medical clowns who operate across the globe, taking their clowning to orphanages in Ethiopia, earthquake victims in Haiti and Nepal, to Houston after Hurricane Irma, to Pittsburgh after the mass shooting in 2018, and more. Working at disaster sites, they help people who are feeling scared, vulnerable, and in pain.

Amnon Raviv, a medical clown, scholar, musician, and theater practitioner was the first to earn a PhD in Medical Clowning in Israel in 2014. His dissertation was about the use of medical clowns with patients who have incurable and life-threatening diseases. He was the first medical clown to work under rocket fire, treating Arab and Israeli shock victims in order to prevent or minimize post-traumatic stress disease (PTSD) symptoms.

Raviv works with geriatric and dialysis patients and conducts research on medical clowning with dementia patients. He was so effective that in 2014, when hospital management decided to discontinue his clown visits to terminal patients due to budget constraints, the patients protested and hundreds wrote letters to management and the media. The media covered the successful overturning of his termination, and subsequently, Raviv led several important studies on laughter.

Fun Facts

There are some delightful fun facts we discovered that don't fit into a neat category. We could have left them out and you would not have missed them. Yet, we believe the creative perspectives on some positive uses of laughter are too fun not to share. They might even elicit a few giggles! Here are a few of the miscellaneous fun facts we unearthed in our quest to put laughter into a larger context for you.

Laughter Saves the Day and the Man

During the 1700s, French writer and public activist, Francois-Marie d'Arouet, best known as Voltaire, wrote, "The art of medicine consists of amusing the patient while nature cures the disease." Voltaire's notion was beautifully illustrated by Dr. William Battie in England in the late 1700s. A young man had an inaccessible abscess in his throat, threatening him with suffocation. All medical options had been exhausted. Dr. Battie made silly faces, set his wig crooked causing laughter, which burst the abscess, saving the patient's life.[37]

First Laughter Club

Kudos to RD Baheti, who founded the *first* Laughter Club in India in 1970. His laughter club did not gain momentum and had limited geographic reach. Regardless, the seed had been planted for what Dr. Madan Kataria would later popularize.

---

37 *Paul Harvey—The Rest of the Story Archive*, "Healing Laughter." https://trotsarchive.com/.

Laughter and Genetics—A Potential to Turn On Your Positive DNA

Can laughter impact our genetics? That question would never have occurred to us, but Kazuo Murakami, one of the top geneticists in the world, was motivated to study the impact of laughter, love, joy, and prayer to activate certain "dormant" genes. His 2006 book, *The Divine Code of Life: Awaken Your Genes & Discover Hidden Talents*, references a study in which he examined the impact of laughter on gene expression.

Professional Laughers

TV sitcoms often had live audiences laughing on the set to help the show feel funnier. Fran Drescher, star of the 1990s sitcom *The Nanny*, was concerned about having random strangers on the set because she had been robbed and assaulted at gunpoint several years prior to the filming. The production team hired professional laughers who were properly screened to be on the show. In interviews shared in the documentary, *Laughology*, many of the professional laughers reported being more relaxed, empathetic, and happier because of laughing every day for years. After the work dried up, many reported experiencing withdrawal and depression.[38] We wonder if forming their own support group to continue laughing together after the show was canceled would have significantly helped them. Their story highlights the valuable power of regular group laughter.

---

38 Albert Nerenberg (Director). (2009). *Laughology*.
    First ever feature documentary about laughter.
    https://youtu.be/B0K5Zwrcf0k?si=aE4BIZr0RLsYL7dB.

Our Most Important Discovery:

LAUGHTER IS AT THE HEART OF EVERYTHING

♥ *After discovering more and more about laughter, it became evident to us that laughter influences every area of life—mental, physical, emotional, and spiritual. No matter where we look, we see laughter making a difference.*

♥ *We created a visual representation of some of the benefits of laughter to help you understand its spectacular impact and vast potential.*

♥ *Look at the laughter touchstones in the illustration, and notice what inspires you to add more purposeful, playful laughter in your life. Use it as a motivational map and see where it takes you.*

♥ *Can you identify advantages of smiling, breathing, playing, or laughing that stimulate you to look for and create more opportunities to add laughter to your life?*

Our Vision of the Future of Laughter

Below we've shared a few ideas about how we envision the laughter-filled world of the future. We hope these imaginings will inspire you and ignite your own creativity as you courageously share the power of laughter with the groups and environments you most want to transform. Imagine...

SCHOOLS

With laughter professionals on staff, schools develop anti-bullying campaigns and train teachers to use Smile-Ups and *Laughter Games* to build connections among students while fostering acceptance and play. Laughter breaks provide ten-minute mini laughter sessions throughout the day to help students and teachers reset and increase focus, productivity, and creative problem-solving. Laughter and clapping can be heard in the halls before and after exams and as transitions between activities. Studies are ongoing to discover the positive impact of a culture rich in purposeful laughter on student and faculty stress levels, student performance, and absenteeism among all students and staff members.

MEDICAL

Dentists and orthodontists infuse education about smiling and laughter into their protocols for oral health and hygiene to provide much needed stress relief for their patients, staff, and themselves. That's just the beginning. Imagine laughter permeating the waiting rooms of all types of health care facilities. Insurance companies offer their own regular laughter sessions and grant premium discounts to those who participate.

SOCIAL WORKERS

Social workers transform people's lives on a global scale by sharing simple laughter techniques and creating regular laughter support groups. We know this is already happening in several places in the United States and England with addiction and recovery as well as other programs.

CAREGIVERS

Caregivers engage patients, asking, "Have you done your Smile-Ups today?" The energy of gentle laughter permeates the halls of hospice centers, senior centers, private homes, and public spaces, as *Laughter Games* are used to help ease pain and stress and replace fear and loneliness with increased connection. Family members and caregivers use laughter on a regular basis for self-care and to address compassion fatigue.

SERVICE INDUSTRY

Wedding planners are trained to implement EGBOK!, Smile-Ups, and Laughter Breaths. While they help couples navigate the stresses of planning a wedding and coping with day-of jitters, they use laughter to prepare newlweds for a lifetime of living together joyfully.

WORK CULTURES

Work cultures incorporate giggles, chuckles, belly laughs, and imaginative play to build stronger teams and cooperation leading to healthier work forces, generating increased productivity and profitability.

JUDGES

Judges send opposing parties to participate in Laughter Yoga sessions prior to mediation to facilitate better feelings and more cooperation between adversarial parties.

And finally, our favorite vision:

LAUGHTER EVERYWHERE

Imagine hearing laughter everywhere you go! Waiting in line or riding an elevator becomes a laughter party. Our unique Laughter Cards are found wherever people gather or conduct business. With laughter directives, quotes, and inspiration, these cards are used to share and spread laughter among friends and strangers, generating instant connections. Easy to follow and fun to use, these cards create an opportunity for people to experience the power and joy of shared laughter.

By the way, Laughter Cards already exist. You can find them on our website:

DISCOVERTHEPOWEROFLAUGHTER.COM

These are our ideas. Where in *your* life would you add smiles and laughter for a joyful, laughter-filled future?

Is there a grin of anticipation plastered on your face? We suspect your heart is eager to spread the discoveries you've made while reading this book, and you are ready to implement some of your own ideas to fill your future with even more laughter.

"The beauty you see in me is a reflection of you."

Rumi, Persian Poet

Conclusion

Laughter Deepens Connection

Twins in the Looking Glass

Rachael

As a child, I remember standing next to Sarah. We were looking at ourselves in the mirror. Except, I was more focused on Sarah's reflection than on my own. As usual, I was looking at Sarah. She said she was a modern witch with supernatural powers like the old television show *Bewitched*. I believed her despite the fact she continually refused to twitch her nose. She also claimed to have powers like Barbara Eden in *I Dream of Jeanie*. I was gullible. I needed to believe her. If *she* had those powers, maybe one day *I* could have them, too. She had created an invisible shield, and I never saw through it because it was so good—so solid. She convinced me she was perfect, invincible, and magic.

I found out, she actually does have magical powers, and it turns out, I have them, too. Wonderful natural powers through laughter. The benefits make it completely worth developing this habit. I've watched Sarah use it for her own benefit all of our lives and especially during the last two decades while sharing the power of laughter with thousands of people.

Sarah believes if she projects something out into the world, it becomes possible. Not *true*, but possible. If she declares she's happy and acts happy, she's going to *become* authentically happy. And, since, like laughter, happiness is also contagious, others around Sarah feel it too.

As I allowed myself to enter Sarah's laughter world, I've discovered it's okay to be like her in some ways without giving up my own identity. The ultimate gift Sarah has given me is positivity and laughter. I am finally able to look in the mirror, laughing and beautiful. I see *myself*.

Sarah

This book started with a desire to share laughter with the world. I wanted to communicate the incredible joy, power, and transformation I've experienced from generating and practicing purposeful, playful laughter. Like many things in life, sharing it with Rachael was not easy for me. While she was carving out her own identity, I was doing the same. Over the years, I never looked past her reflection in the mirror to see the things I now recognize as her unique gifts. As a result, I missed out on some of the best parts of her.

I'll keep putting joy and laughter into my life even when the challenges feel overwhelming. It works for me. Life is never quite so bad as I thought a few minutes before I decide to add laughter—whether I'm dealing with a broken glass, a broken relationship, or whatever else life throws my way. I truly hope this will become your experience, too.

Laughter is a safe space to find common ground, even for people who are at odds. Rachael and I don't see eye to eye on many things that might drive a wedge between people in ordinary relationships—from religion, to politics, to how many footnotes are too many in a book. Our collaboration was born out of a desire to bring laughter to you, the reader. Through equal parts shared laughter, play, and frustration, we rediscovered ourselves and each other.

Laughter puts me in the present. When I choose to laugh out loud, time is suspended. My current problem temporarily fades, replaced by joyful giggles. The problem no longer holds the power. The joy allows me to see life differently. It works remarkably well. We can't wait to hear what practicing hearty laughter does for you.

Final Meditation

You now possess the knowledge and tools to shift your mindset, add positivity, and laugh whenever you choose. With self-discovery you have awakened childhood curiosity. Hesitation and resistance have melted away, at least for moments. We are excited to think of you designing your own personal playground of laughter.

It is our sincere hope laughter will soon become your most treasured healthy habit. We trust you will take it with you toward an empowered, healthy, and joy-filled life.

Inhale.

Take a slow,

deep breath.

*With your hands on your heart
feel our gratitude for the time you spent
learning and laughing with us.*

It's been an incredible journey.

*Celebrate the love and joy of our shared
laughter spilling out into the world.*

Alphabetical List of *Laughter Games*

Catch the Giggles   99

Celebrate Your Accomplishments Laugh   159

Childhood Memories at the Beach   149

Clapping Games
   Ho-Ho! Ha-Ha-Ha!   92
   Very Good, Very Good, Yay!   93
   Favorite Language   94

Cleansing the Negativity   128

Everything's Gonna Be O-Kay! (EGBOK!)   152

Finger Skipping   64

Gentle Finger Laughter   146

Gradient Laughter   192

Gratitude Laughter   156

Grin & Bear It, or . . . The Grim Grin Trim   122

Hold Hands and Laugh   184

I Love Myself Laugh   97

The Inner Critic Meets the Laughter Lover   127

Jokes by Number   195

Joyful Giggles   87

Laugh in Color   101

Laughter Breaths   52

Laughter-Infused Boots   110

Laughter Meditation   102

The Perfect Pivot   154

Put On Your Laughter Glasses   124

Put Up Your Laughter Shield   134

Shoe Shopping with Laughter   111

Shower Yourself with Laughter   96

Silent Laughter   100

Smile-Ups   42

Swing Like a Child and Play   60

Unzip Your Smile   90

WYHa20 (**W**ash **Y**our **Ha**nds for **20** seconds)   153

Who's Tapping on Your Shoulder?   130

Laughter Games to Boost Health & Joy

For your convenience we've created this *Quick Reference Guide,* categorizing the *Laughter Games.* Have fun creating different combinations. Start with a few warm-ups, include transitions and breathing as needed. Relax with a Laughter Meditation.

> **REMEMBER**
> - Make Eye Contact—even if you use a mirror or your imagination.
> - Accept yourself and others—you've got this!

WARM-UPS

- Smile-Ups 42
- Unzip Your Smile 90
- Laughter Breaths 52
- Deep Belly Breathing (*Jump Start*) 51
- Joyful Giggles 87

PLAYFUL TRANSITIONS (WITH CLAPPING)

- Ho-Ho! Ha-Ha-Ha! 92
- *Very Good, Very Good, Yay!* and Yippee! 93
- Italian + other foreign language versions 94

GENTLE *Laughter Games*

- Gentle Finger Laughter 146
- Finger Skipping 64
- Childhood Memories at the Beach 149
- Gratitude Laughter 156
- Silent Laughter 100

SELF-CARE TO BUILD CONFIDENCE

- WYHa20 (**W**ash **Y**our **H**ands for **20** seconds) 153
- Shower Yourself with Laughter 96
- The Inner Critic Meets the Laughter Lover 127
- Cleansing the Negativity 128
- I Love Myself Laugh 97

Laughter Games to Boost Health and Joy

STRESS MANAGEMENT

- Everything's Gonna Be O-Kay! (EGBOK!) 152
- Grin & Bear It, or . . . The Grim Grin Trim 122
- Who's Tapping on Your Shoulder? 130
- Put Up Your Laughter Shield 134

SHIFT YOUR PERSPECTIVE

- Put on Your Laughter Glasses 124
- The Perfect Pivot 154
- Laugh in Color 101
- Laughter-Infused Boots 110
- Shoe Shopping with Laughter 111

COLLABORATION AND PARTNERSHIP

- Catch the Giggles 99
- Jokes by Number 195
- Hold Hands and Laugh 184

CELEBRATIONS & FUN

- Gradient Laughter 192
- Celebrate Your Accomplishments Laugh 159
- Swing Like a Child and Play 60

GRAND FINALE

- Laughter Meditation 102

By no means are the *Laughter Games* in this book an exhaustive list. They're merely a taste. Our list constantly grows and changes. You never know when a newly created game will become a long-standing favorite. Experiment. Keep it fresh and fun.

Visit our website regularly to find more games. Website:

DiscoverThePowerOfLaughter.com

Additional Resources

We're sharing what we believe to be fun, fascinating, and useful references to satisfy a variety of interests. Among the treasures here, you'll find a few specific gems we want you to have—a free pdf book about play, a full-length documentary about laughter, and the names of books for children that Sarah used with Jacqueline during her hospital stay. In addition, we hope you'll find topics and items of interest to jump-start your own laughter discoveries.

Business & Success

Achor, Shawn. *The Happiness Advantage: How a Positive Brain Fuels Success in Work and in Life.* (New York: Crown Business, 2010).

Clear, James. *Atomic Habits: Tiny Changes, Remarkable Results, An Easy & Proven Way to Build Good Habits & Break Bad Ones.* (New York: Avery, imprint of Penguin Random House, 2018).

Herman, Todd. *The Alter Ego Effect: The Power of Secret Identities to Transform Your Life.* (New York: Harper Business imprint of HarperCollins Publishers, 2019).

Magdino, Og. *The Greatest Salesman in the World: You Can Change Your Life with the Priceless Wisdom of Ten Ancient Scrolls Handed Down for Thousands of Years*. (New York: Bantam Books, 1968).

Stanhope, Philip Dormer, 4th Earl of Chesterfield. (1694-1773) *Letters to His Son on the Fine Art of Becoming a Man of the World and a Gentleman*. This book, now in the public domain, can be found online in its entirety thanks to David Widger and Project Gutenberg eBooks. https://www.gutenberg.org/ebooks/3361

TEDGlobal. "Your Body Language May Shape who You Are | Amy Cuddy | TEDGlobal," June 2012. https://www.ted.com/talks/amy_cuddy_your_body_language_may_shape_who_you_are?subtitle=en

Children

Addyman, Caspar, PhD. *The Laughing Baby: The Extraordinary Science Behind What Makes Babies Happy*. (London: Unbound, 2020).

Garth, Maureen. *Moonbeam: A Book of Meditations for Children*. (New York: HarperOne, 1st edition, 1993).

Garth, Maureen. *Starbright Meditations for Children*. (New York: HarperSanFrancisco, a Division of HarperCollins Publishers, 1991).

Gold, Roberta, R.T.C., CHP. (2018). *The Family that Laughs Together: A Quick Guide to Sanity When You Feel Like Screaming*. (Independently Published: Laughter for the Health of It, 2018).

Lee, Ingrid Fetell. "The Navajo Celebration of a Baby's First Laugh." *The Aesthetics of Joy,* May 22, 2020. https://aestheticsofjoy.com/navajo-celebration-babys-first-laugh/

Michelli, Jospeh, PhD. *Humor, Play & Laughter: Stress-Proofing Life with Your Kids.* (Colorado: Love and Logic Press, Inc., 1998).

Morrison, Mary Kay. *Legacy of Laughter: A Grandparent Guide & Playbook.* (Salem, New Hampshire: Free People Publishing, 2021).

Education

Loomans, Diana and Karen Kolberg. *The Laughing Classroom: Everyone's Guide to Teaching with Humor and Play.* (California: New World Library, Fifth Printing edition, 2002).

Nazari, Amir Mohamad, Mohammad Javad Ghazanfari, Amir Emami Zeydi, and Akbar Zare-Kaseb. "The Effect of Laughter Yoga on Stress and Anxiety of Nursing Students: A Systematic Review." *Teaching and Learning in Nursing,* Feb 2024. https://www.sciencedirect.com/science/article/abs/pii/S1557308724000313.

Savage, Brandon M., Heidi L. Lujan, Raghavendar R. Thipparthi, and Stephen E. DiCarlo. "Humor Laughter, Learning, and Health! A Brief Review." *Advances in Physiology Education.* 2017; 41: 341-347. https://journals.physiology.org/doi/epdf/10.1152/advan.00030.2017

Grief & Loss

Abramson, Nikki, and Barbara Hynes-Tomczyk. *Anthology Can't Somebody Fix What Ails Me? 21 Stories of Chronic Illness.* (US: NB Productions, 2020).

Lund Dale A., PhD, Rebecca Utz, PhD, Michael S. Caserta, PhD, and Briande Vries, PhD. "Humor, Laughter & Happiness in the Daily Lives of Recently Bereaved Spouses." *Omega (Westport),* 2008; 58(2): 87-105. https://www.ncbi.nlm.nih.gov/pmc/articles/PMC2646184/pdf/nihms53706.pdf

Mendoza, Marilyn A., PhD. "The Healing Power of Laughter in Death and Grief: Humor in Hospice." *Psychology Today,* (November 7, 2016) https://www.psychologytoday.com/intl/blog/understanding-grief/201611/the-healing-power-laughter-in-death-and-grief

Wilson, Donna M., Kathleen Bykowski, Ana M. Chrzanowski, Michelle Knox, and Begoña Errasti-Ibarrondo. "A Scoping Research Literature Review to Explore Bereavement Humor." *Current Psychology,* (2022). https://www.ncbi.nlm.nih.gov/pmc/articles/PMC8975707/pdf/12144_2022_Article_3033.pdf

Health

Laughter & Health Overview

Cousins, Norman. *Anatomy of an Illness as Perceived by the Patient.* (New York: W.W. Norton & Company, 1979).

> For a comprehensive discussion with many resources, look at: Gendry, Sebastian. "Benefits of Laughter: The Ultimate Cheat Sheet," *Laughter Online University.* https://www.laughteronlineuniversity.com/benefits-of-laughter/

Louie, Dexter, BA, Brook Carolina, MD, and Elizabeth Frates, MD. "The Laughter Prescription: A Tool for Lifestyle Medicine." *American Journal of Lifestyle Medicine,* (July/August 2016). https://www.ncbi.nlm.nih.gov/pmc/articles/PMC6125057/pdf/10.1177_1559827614550279.pdf

Mora-Ripoll, Ramon. "Potential health benefits of simulated laughter: A narrative review of the literature and recommendations for future research." *Complimentary Therapies in Medicine,*" Vol 19, 3 June 2011, 170-177. Laughter Research Network, Barcelona, Spain. https://www.sciencedirect.com/science/article/abs/pii/S0965229911000574

Shapiro, Sarah. *An Audience of One and Other Stories.* (New York: Mosaica Press, 2021).

Walsh, James, MD. *Laughter and Health.* (New York: D. Appleton & Company, 1928).

Addiction & Recovery

Coleman, Slash, MA Ed. "Redefining Addiction and Recovery Through Laughter Yoga." *Psychology Today,* October 29, 2019. https://www.psychologytoday.com/us/blog/bohemian-love-diaries/201910/redefining-addiction-and-recovery-through-laughter-yoga

Cancer

> We found this Korean study of laughter's impact on breast cancer patients important because of how little laughter it takes to have a positive effect. We've quoted from the study here:
>
> Conclusion: [Note: TLP = Therapeutic Laughter Program]
>
> "The TLP is effective in reducing anxiety, depression, and stress in breast cancer patients, and such *effects can be attained after only one session* [emphasis ours]. This study is useful as there has been little previous analysis of the effect of the number of TLP sessions. TLP could also be used effectively in clinical practice settings, as it is a noninvasive, easy-to-use complementary/alternative therapy; therefore, it is recommended that medical professionals use a standardized TLP as a complementary intervention to assist with patient treatment."
>
> Kim, S.H., Y.H. Kim, and H. J. Kim. "Laughter and Stress Relief in Cancer Patients: A Pilot Study." Hindawi Publishing Corporation. *Evidence-Based Complementary and Alternative Medicine*, Volume 2015, Article ID 864739, 6 pages, 2015. http://dx.doi.org/10.1155/2015/864739

Penson, Richard T., Rosamund A. Partridge, Pandora Rudd, Michael V. Seiden, Jill E. Nelson, Bruce A. Chabner, and Thomas J. Lynch. "Update: Laughter: The Best Medicine?" *The Oncologist* 10, no. 8 (September 1, 2005): 651–60. https://doi.org/10.1634/theoncologist.10-8-651.

In this 2024 meta-analysis (below), laughter modalities, including Laughter Yoga, clown interventions, and watching humorous movies, were examined for their effectiveness in impacting negative emotions such as depression, anxiety, stress, pain, and fatigue.

Shi, Hongyu, Yuejin Wu, Lu Wang, Xiuling Zhou, and Feng Li. "Effects of Laughter Therapy on Improving Negative Emotions Associated with Cancer: A Systematic Review and Meta-Analysis." *Oncology* 102, no. 4 (October 31, 2023): 343–53. https://doi.org/10.1159/000533690.

Rothberg, Saranne, Stage IV Cancer survivor, hosts an uplifting podcast, *Beating Cancer Daily*. https://www.comedycures.org/bcdpodcast

Turner, Kelly A., PhD. *Radical Remission: the Nine Key Factors That Can make a Real Difference, Surviving Cancer Against All Odds*. (New York: Harper One, Harper Collins Publishers, 2014).

Diabetes

In August 2023, *Frontiers in Endocrinology* published an editorial on research topics in clinical diabetes entitled, "Influence of Lifestyle Factors in the Management of Diabetes Mellitus." One of the included research articles examined a 12-week Laughter Yoga program for its feasibility for individuals with type 2 diabetes.

Hirosaki, Mayumi, Tetsuya Ohira, Yawei Wu, Eri Eguchi, Kokoro Shirai, Hironori Imano, Narumi Funakubo, et al. "Laughter Yoga as an Enjoyable Therapeutic Approach for Glycemic Control in Individuals With Type 2 Diabetes: A Randomized Controlled Trial." *Frontiers in Endocrinology* 14 (March 31, 2023). https://doi.org/10.3389/fendo.2023.1148468.

Napora, Joseph P., PhD., LCSW-C. *Stress-Free Diabetes: Your Guide to Health and Happiness*. (Virginia: American Diabetes Association, 2010).

Heart Health

European Society of Cardiology Press Release quoting Dr. Michael Miller, "Laughter Has a Positive Impact on Vascular Function," (April 28, 2011). https://www.escardio.org/The-ESC/Press-Office/Press-releases/Laughter-has-a-positive-impact-on-vascular-function

Hayashi, Kei, Ichiro Karachi, Tetsuya Ohira, Katsunori Kondo, Kokoro Shirai, and Naoki Kondo. "Laughter Is the Best Medicine? A Cross-Sectional Study of Cardiovascular Disease Among Older Japanese Adults." *Journal of Epidemiology* 26, no. 10 (January 1, 2016): 546–52. https://pmc.ncbi.nlm.nih.gov/articles/PMC5037252/pdf/je-26-546.pdf

Miller, Michael, MD, with Catherine Knepper. *Heal Your Heart: The Positive Emotions Prescription To Prevent and Reverse Heart Disease*. (Pennsylvania: Rodale, Inc., 2014).

Wooten, Patty, RN. *Heart, Humor & Healing*. (California: Jest Press, 1994).

History

Court Jesters

Otto, Beatrice K. *Fools are Everywhere: the Court Jester Around the World*. (Chicago: The University of Chicago Press, 2007).

Documentary About Laughter

> Nerenberg, Albert (Director). (2009). *Laughology*. First ever feature documentary about laughter. Available in its entirety online. https://youtube.com/watch?v=B0K5Zwrcf0k.

General History

Jones, Peter J. A. *Laughter and Power in the Twelfth Century*. (Oxford University Press, 2019).

Serious Science. "The History of Laughter — Peter Jones / Serious Science," March 24, 2020. https://www.youtube.com/watch?v=RQdf4Riwp0E.

Sully, James. *Essay on Laughter, Its Causes, Its Development and Its Value*. (London: Longmans, Green and Co., 1902).

Philosophy of Humor

Morreall, John. *Comic Relief: A Comprehensive Philosophy of Humor (New Directions in Aesthetics, No. 9)*. Part of *New Directions in Aesthetics* (10 books). (Oxford: Wiley-Blackwell, a John Wiley & Sons, Ltd., Publication, 2009).

Vasey, George. *The Philosophy of Laughter and Smiling*. (London: J. Burns, 1875).

Humor & Health

*Humor and Laughter May Influence Health—
A Review of the Evidence*

A four-part series reviewing the evidence of how humor influences physiological and psychological well-being:

Bennett, M.P., and C.A. Lengacher. "Humor and Laughter May Influence Health: I. History and Background." *Evidence-Based Complementary and Alternative Medicine*, 2006; 3(1): 61-63. https://www.ncbi.nlm.nih.gov/pmc/articles/PMC1375238/pdf/nek015.pdf

Bennett, M.P., and C.A. Lengacher. "Humor and Laughter May Influence Health: II. Complementary Therapies and Humor in a Clinical Population." *Evidence-Based Complementary and Alternative Medicine*, 2006;3(2): 187-190. https://onlinelibrary.wiley.com/doi/epdf/10.1093/ecam/nel014

Bennett, M.P., and C.A. Lengacher "Humor and Laughter May Influence Health: III. Laughter and Health Outcomes." *Evidence-Based Complementary and Alternative Medicine*, 2008;5(1): 37-40 https://downloads.hindawi.com/journals/ecam/2008/904752.pdf

Bennett, M.P., and C.A. Lengacher. "Humor and Laughter May Influence Health IV. Humor and Immune Function." *Evidence-Based Complementary and Alternative Medicine*, 2009;6(2): 159-164. https://www.ncbi.nlm.nih.gov/pmc/articles/PMC2686627/pdf/nem149.pdf.

Klein, Allen. *The Healing Power of Humor: Techniques for Getting through Loss, Setbacks, Upsets, Disappointments, Difficulties, Trials, Tribulations, and All That Not-So-Funny Stuff.* (New York: Jeremy P. Tarcher/Putnam a member of Penguin Putnam, Inc., 1989).

Morreall, John, PhD. *Humor Works.* (Massachusetts: HRD Press, 1997).

An article that reviews and analyzes a variety of research on the therapeutic effects of laughter and humor is:

Van der Wal, Natalie, C., and Robin N. "Laughter-Inducing Therapies: Systematic Review and Meta-Analysis." *Social Science & Medicine,* 232 (July 1, 2019), 473-488. https://doi.org/10.1016/j.socscimed.2019.02.018

Medical Clowns

Raviv, Amnon, PhD. *Medical Clowning: The Healing Performance.* (London New York Calcutta: Seagull Books, 2018).

Raviv, Amnon, PhD. *New Perspectives on Medical Clowning: Clown Doctors in Covid-19, Wartime, and the Everyday.* (New York: Routledge, an imprint of the Taylor & Francis Group, 2023).

Joy

Altman, Donald. *The Joy Compass: 8 Ways to Find Lasting Happiness, Gratitude & Optimism in the Present Moment.* (New York: MJF Books, 2012).

Shore, Barry. *The Joy of Living: How to Slay Stress and Be Happy.* (California: Joy of Living Institute Publishing, 2021). Available as a paperback and as a FREE download at https://barryshore.com/ebook/. Enjoy his podcast, *The Joy of Living*. Find our episode: "Laugh Your Way to Health Wealth Wisdom."

Laughter Yoga Books & Practitioners

Of the hundreds of laughter professionals worldwide, we've included here those who have inspired us, both with their own books, as well as our personal experiences learning and laughing with them. The resources, including laughter videos they share, are well worth your exploration. You will be enriched by whatever experience you may have as you delve deeper.

We are constantly discovering new people. Use these resources as a jump start for your own laughter journey.

Berman, Dave & Kelly T. Woods. *Laughter for the Health of It.* (SC: Dave Berman & Kelly Woods, 2015).

Briar, Jeffrey. *Laughter Mastery: Laughter Yoga Training and Advanced Education.* (California: Creative Arts Press, 2017).

Briar, Jeffrey. *The Laughter Yoga Book: Laugh Yourself to Better Health Physical Mental Emotional Social Spiritual.* (The Laughter Yoga Institute: Create Space Independent Publishing Platform, 2016).

Kataria, Madan, MD. *Laugh for No Reason.* (Mumbai: Madhuri International, 1999).

Lyle, Lesley. *Laugh Your Way to Happiness: Use The Science of Laughter for Total Well-Being.* (London: Watkins Publishing, 2014).

Sturge, Lisa. *Laugh: Everyday Laughter Healing for Greater Happiness and Wellbeing.* (Quadrille Publishing, 2017).

Merv Neal is Australia's leading laughter expert who focuses on workplace wellness. Discover what he's doing in Australia at https://www.mervneal.com

Robert Rivest has created a treasure trove of YouTube videos as well as the Rivest method of Joyful Living at https://wellbeinglaughter.com/

Sebastian Gendry is a recognized leader in the laughter wellness community. We've learned from and laughed with Sebastian and found his many contributions compelling. Explore his vast research and experience at https://www.SebastianGendry.com.

Mental Health

Üner, Elif, Ayşe Sezer Balcı, Hasibe Kadıoğlu. "The Effect of Laughter Therapy on Physical and Mental Health: Systematic Review." *Journal of Public Health Nursing,* 4(3) (2022): 251-269. https://dergipark.org.tr/en/download/article-file/2371755.

Yim, Jongen. "Therapeutic Benefits of Laughter in Mental Health: A Theoretical Review." *The Tohoku Journal of Experimental Medicine,* 239, no. 3 (January 1, 2016): 243–49. https://www.jstage.jst.go.jp/article/tjem/239/3/239_243/_pdf/-char/en.

Personal Development

Coleman, Slash. *Laugh for Life: 5 Extraordinary and Extremely Easy Ways to Improve Your Laugh Life.* (VA: Laugh for Life Publishing, 2020).

Davies, Stephanie. *Laughology: Improve Your Life with the Science of Laughter.* (Wales: Crown House Publishing, Ltd., 2013).

Goodman, Joel. *Laffirmations: 1,001 Ways to Add Humor to Your Life and Work.* (Florida: Health Communications, Inc., 1995).

Murakami, Kazuo, PhD. *The Divine Code of Life: Awaken Your Genes & Discover Hidden Talents.* (Beyond Words Publishing, Inc., 2006).

Play

Brown, Stuart, MD, & Christopher Vaughan. *Play: How it Shapes the Brain, Opens the Imagination and Invigorates the Soul.* (New York: Avery, Penguin Group Inc, 2009).

> DeKoven, Bernard. *A Playful Path.* (ETC Press, 2014). Available as a paperback and as a FREE download at www.aplayfulpath.com.

Eastman, Max. *The Enjoyment of Laughter.* (London: Routledge, 2009).

> We found it fun to explore the National Institute for Play website at https://nifplay.org

Relationships

Cunningham, Ted. *A Love That Laughs: Lighten Up, Cut Loose and Enjoy Life Together.* (Illinois: Tyndale House Publishers, 2020).

Junkins, Enda, LCSW. *Belly Laughter & Relationships: Something Else Positive Below the Belt.* (Texas: Dustin Royale Publishers, 2002).

Research

Early research involving laughter focused primarily on humor or used humor to generate the laughter being studied. Since the beginning of the twenty-first century, research has been conducted to move beyond humor and specifically study the effectiveness of purposeful laughter without humor. In these studies, the laughter is called: Laughter Yoga, The Laughter Program, simulated, or intentional laughter. Here are a few interesting studies:

American Physiological Society. "Anticipating A Laugh Reduces Our Stress Hormones, Study Shows." *ScienceDaily*. (April 10, 2008). https://www.sciencedaily.com/releases/2008/04/080407114617.htm (accessed May 13, 2024).

Berk, Lee S., MPH, Dr. PH, David L. Felten, MD, PhD, Stanley A. Tan, MD, PhD, Barry B. Bittman, ME, and James Westergard, BS. "Modulation of Neuroimmune Parameters During the Eustress of Humor-Associated Mirthful Laughter." *Alternative Therapies in Health and Medicine,* 2001;7(2): 62-76.

Byrd, Alita. "World Authority on Laughter Talks Us Through the Research." *Spectrum* magazine, (August 9, 2015). https://spectrummagazine.org/views/interviews/world-authority-laughter-talks-us-through-research/

Kramer, C. K., and C. B. Leitao. "Laughter as Medicine: A Systematic Review and Meta-Analysis of Interventional Studies Evaluating the Impact of Spontaneous Laughter on Cortisol Levels." *PLoS ONE* 18, no. 5 (May 23, 2023): e0286260. https://www.ncbi.nlm.nih.gov/pmc/articles/PMC10204943/

The article below acknowledges three decades of research by Canadian academic, Professor Rod Martin, who specialized in clinical psychology and humor research.

Kuiper, Nicholas A. "Three Decades Investigating Humor and Laughter. An interview with Professor Rod Martin." *Europe's Journal of Psychology,* 2016;12(3):498-512. https://www.ncbi.nlm.nih.gov/pmc/articles/PMC4991054/pdf/ejop-12-498.pdf

Provine, Robert R., PhD. *Laughter: A Scientific Investigation.* (New York: Penguin Books, 2000).

TEDx Talks. "Why We Should Take Laughter More Seriously | Sophie Scott | TEDxExeter," June 7, 2018. https://www.youtube.com/watch?v=TKYwGYrVm0o.

Seniors

Gonot-Schoupinsky, F.N., and G. Garip, "Laughter and Humour Interventions for Well-Being in Older Adults: A Systematic Review and Intervention Classification." *Complementary Therapies in Medicine,* 2018;(38): 85-91. https://www.sciencedirect.com/science/article/abs/pii/S0965229918302358

Ghodsbin, Fariba, MSc, Zahra Sharif Ahmadi, BS, Iran Jahanbin, MSc, Farkhondeh Sharif, PhD. "The Effects of Laughter Therapy on General Health of Elderly People Referring to Jahandidegan Community Center in Shiraz, Iran, 2014: A Randomized Controlled Trial." *International Journal Community Based Nurse Midwifery,* 2015 Jan;3(1): 31-38. https://www.ncbi.nlm.nih.gov/pmc/articles/PMC4280555/pdf/ijcbnm-3-31.pdf

Greene, Celeste, MA, Jennifer Craft Morgan, PhD, LaVona S. Traywick, PhD, Chivon A. Mingo, PhD. "Evaluation of a Laughter-based Exercise Program on Health and Self-Efficacy for Exercise." *The Gerontologist,* December 2017;57(6): 1051-1061. https://doi.org/10.1093/geront/gnw105

Spirituality

Sparks, Reverend Susan. *Laugh Your Way to Grace: Reclaiming the Spiritual Power of Humor.* (Vermont: Sky Light Paths Publishing, 2010).

Stolik, Gitty. *It's Okay to Laugh Seriously!: A Spiritual Perspective.* (Israel: Mosaica Press, Inc., 2016).

We mentioned Waraiko, the Japanese Laughter Ceremony, and were delighted to discover a video showing the participants laughing. "800-Year-Old Laughing Festival in Yamaguchi Perf." https://www.gettyimages.com/detail/video/waraiko-a-rare-festival-in-which-residents-laugh-off-the-news-footage/460263972

Stress

Gendry, Sebastian. "How to Manage Stress the Fun Way." https://www.laughteronlineuniversity.com/how-to-manage-stress/.

Goodheart, Annette, PhD. *Laughter Therapy: How To Laugh About Everything in Your Life that Isn't Really Funny.* (Santa Barbara, California: Less Stress Press, 1994).

Hatchard, Anna, and Piers Worth. "No Laughing Matter: Qualitative Study of the Impact of Laughter Yoga Suggests Stress Innoculation." "Volume 5, Article 2 – European Journal of Applied Positive Psychology," n.d. https://www.nationalwellbeingservice.org/volumes/volume-5-2021/volume-5-article-2/.

Lefcourt, Herbert M., and Rod A. Martin. *Humor and Life Stress: Antidote to Adversity.* (New York: Springer, 1986).

Meier, Maria, Lisa Wirz, Philip Dickinson, and Jens C. Pruessner. "Laughter Yoga Reduces the Cortisol Response to Acute Stress in Healthy Individuals." *Stress* 24, no. 1 (May 26, 2020): 44–52. https://doi.org/10.1080/10253890.2020.1766018.

Selye, Hans, MD. *The Stress of Life.* Revised Edition. (New York: McGraw-Hill Companies, Inc., 1978).

Survival

Gonzales, Laurence. *Deep Survival: Who Lives, Who Dies, and Why.* (New York: W.W. Norton & Company, 2003).

Well-Being

Ellis-Young, Laurie, and George T. Ellis, PsyD. *Breath Is Life: Taking in and Letting Go, How to Live Well, Love Well, BE Well.* (Minneapolis: Breathe the Change Press, 2021).

Gendry, Sebastian, "Clapping Hands Can Change Your Life: Science, Testimonial, Video." *Laughter Online University.* https://www.laughteronlineuniversity.com/clapping-hands/

King, Dr. Brian. *The Laughing Cure: Emotional and Physical Healing—A Comedian Reveals Why Laughter Really Is the Best Medicine.* (New York: Skyhorse Publishing, 2016).

Prilleltensky, Isaac. *The Laughing Guide to Well-Being: Using Humor and Science to Become Happier and Healthier.* (Maryland: Rowman and Littlefield, 2016).

Greater Good. "How Nature Can Make You Kinder, Happier, and More Creative," March 2, 2016. https://greatergood.berkeley.edu/article/item/how_nature_makes_you_kinder_happier_more_creative.

Gono-Schoupinksy, Freda N., Merv Neal, and Jerome Carson. "Is Laughter Really the Best Medicine? Reflecting on a Mental Health Initiative Using Pragmatic Collaborative Autoethnography." *Journal of Applied Social Science* 18, no. 1 (August 29, 2023): 19–31. https://doi.org/10.1177/19367244231195059.

Laughter Games

Find the *Laughter Games* included in this book on our website and check often for new games:

DiscoverThePowerOfLaughter.com

Behind the Scenes & Acknowledgments

Our journey began in the living room with Sarah engaged in a deep and personal conversation with Rachael's son, Levi. It continued until all the dots were connected, forming the impetus for this book. Levi's curiosity, patience, and persistence led back to the important memories of Jacqueline in the hospital that were aching to be shared with the world. His acknowledgement, validation, and encouragement for Sarah to share her story were pivotal. Our gratitude and appreciation to Levi know no bounds.

Joshua Bains literally launched our foray into the editing process with his thoughtful questions, resources, and guidance. He made our work fun, kept our voices, and improved our writing. He suggested we explore inhibitions and resistance to laughter and urged us to look deeply into our experiences to discover the source of what came to be a key element of the book. We are so grateful.

Thanks to Slash Coleman for his time, attention, and honest feedback. He guided us toward serious soul-searching and motivated us to break through our own barriers and become more vulnerable so we could make the difference we are committed to making in the world. His generosity, candor, and insightful feedback significantly influenced the core and essence of this book.

We want to recognize the many laughter professionals who unwittingly planted the seeds that brought life to this book. In addition, everyone who has intentionally laughed with us in person, over the phone, or online has kept us fresh and on our toes throughout the entire book-writing process. We are especially grateful to Wala Al-Daraji, Marie Cocozzello, Tsivya Frieder, Lou Hopson, Miriam Hammelburger, Esther Kletter, Mercedes Mack, Judi Olson, Saranne Rothberg, Maria Maria Sangria, Chana Spanier, Joan Stiles, and Jill Widness who inspired new *Laughter Games* and whose support and contributions have impacted our laughter work in creative and positive ways and uplifted us as human beings.

We are forever grateful to Patricia Moreno and Lucy Osborne for their programs, *Sati365* and *The Evolution*, during which Rachael was inspired to create the Laughter Breath game and her Declaration of a Laughter Champion.

As dear friends who gave so generously of their time and skills, Alexandra Carrara, Galit Gottlieb, Bev Fermon, Joseph Rosenthal, and Adina Simon offered thought-provoking feedback that led us to rethink, reimagine, and ultimately reshape the reader's experience. We are deeply grateful to each of them for their care and gentle handling of our ideas and words. Our book would truly not be what it is without each of them.

An enormous thank-you to our beta readers, some of whom read more than one version of the book, and many who helped us narrow down the title and the cover which were no small tasks. Each piece of feedback we received was considered and incorporated to elevate our message. We so appreciate you: Carol Allis, Joel Alpert, Arlene Appelrouth, Michele Asa, Leanne Benson, Jeni Caplan, Clair Carpenter, Jodie Cohen, Phyllis Dozier, Jaime Esshaghian, Laurie Ellis-Young, Christian Fernandes, Adam Fillary, Rachel Foody, Cherryl Galezewski, Stephanie Goldberg, Yacova Guigui, Sheva Habif, Viktor Haimov, Lou Hopson, Jai Dei Jackson, Katia Kulyk, Chana Marcus, David Matthews, Phyllis McNabb, Lisa Metwaly, Kathy Nagy, Patience Nallick, Mecca Page, Michael Precker, Dr. Deborah Rosenthal, Maria Maria Sangria, Robin Saul, Shoshana Siegelman, Dorothy Sinha, Dr. Drew Southerland, Rachel Stein, Denny Stockdale, and Yehudit Stupnicker. Lisa Yvonne of Fernhead Publishing offered her support and guidance from the beginning. We are filled with gratitude for the members of Sarah's writing group, Women of Words (WOW), and especially Nancy Chakrin who offered her wisdom and connections.

Many capable professionals touched our book on its journey: Herta Fecly, from Chrysalis Editorial, Dayna Haimot, Lyda Haerle and Mike Nicloy of Nico 11 Publishing & Design, Mecca Page, Mary Rains, Colleen Sell, and Jodi Svgar. Each of them impacted our book-writing adventure in unique ways, making sure we took our time and delivered our very best work.

We appreciate everyone, named and unnamed, who contributed thoughts, questions, insights, and offered encouragement along the way.

What we've both learned from our collective laughter experience could more than fill a book. *(Ha-Ha!)* We are grateful for every lesson learned, every shared laugh, and every single edit. All of them. We mean it. One day we'll share the outtakes.

Memories of Peggy's unique laugh permeate our hearts. Jacqueline's peals of laughter surround us and fill the pages of this book. The sounds of Grandpa Barney's *Yippee!* cheer us on continuously. Their energy lives on in us, and we are humbled to share it with you, our readers.

We are forever in awe of our parents, Connie and Stanley Blum, for the relationship they have, and have modeled since we can remember. We cherish their continuous love and support.

Our younger sister Julie holds a special place in each of our hearts. Her willingness to listen, provide feedback, and guide us towards better writing and better living has helped each of us become who we are.

Sarah

You never know where a simple action is going to lead. Everything has a way of falling into place, coming together just where it belongs. Yet, we always choose which path to take at the crossroads, and oh, what a difference it can make.

I did not know that I needed to write *this* book. When I set out to write a book about laughter it was a very different book. Long after my initial conversation with my nephew, Levi, about Jacqueline's life, I came to understand the difference that conversation made for me on multiple levels.

I didn't realize until recently that the road to writing this book at all was in large part paved by three incredible human beings: Dr. Terry Harville, Jacqueline's primary doctor, who communicated from the very first afternoon he spent with us that we were not 'just another patient' to him; Ninna Burkill, the Child Life Specialist who guided Jacqueline and Monica through both bone marrow transplants and was with Jacqueline during her most critical moments when I was not allowed to be; and Michelle Roos, a college student when we first met, who helped me create and later continued—*For Parents Only,* a program to support the parents of hospitalized kids. The difference each of them made, not just in my life, but in my entire approach to Jacqueline's life, her care, and my ability to live with her in the hospital, take care of my other children, and live in the world even after Jacqueline died, is hard to articulate. Not only did Terry, Ninna, and Michelle become my friends, but the relationships I was able to have with them and all the nurses, doctors, and caregivers in the three hospitals where Jacqueline spent time, helped me to feel normal during a very stressful time and in abnormal environments. I did not know it then, but I know now that Jacqueline and I would never have had the experiences in the hospital we did, and I would never have written this book or learned to navigate the world again after Jacqueline died, were it not for their genuine love, concern, and sheer kindness. I don't know how to acknowledge the gifts they gave me that ultimately opened up a space that led to the sharing of my story and the writing of this book.

Allison and Monica, my two incredible daughters, have brought me more love than I can ever express. My grandson, Ethan, has brought a new light to my life. In his smiles and laughter, I find the same joy and wonder that Jacqueline taught me so long ago. I count myself the luckiest person alive.

Just minutes before I entered the world, my twin sister Rachael cleared the path to make way for me. Co-authoring this book is merely the most recent way she has supported me and lifted me up in ways well beyond what I feel I deserve. We don't see eye to eye on so many things, and yet, we share a special bond that discovering the power of laughter together has only strengthened. I would not be who I am without her. I can never express my gratitude enough.

Rachael

In my view, it all starts with G-d.*
He gave us the gift of laughter in the first place.
He made us twins, chose our grandfather, our cousin Peggy, and Jacqueline with her illness.
He created detrusor muscles and bladders.
He created the full spectrum of human emotions.
I am eternally grateful to Him for all His gifts and blessings.

My life wouldn't be the same if not for the enlightened guidance, care, and friendship of Sylvia Sultenfuss and Alexandra Carrara, who helped me understand myself and the world in ways that helped me come closer to finding my purpose in the world and my striving to fulfill it. A special appreciation to my good friend Yacova Guigui who sustains me and shares this journey with me. Having people who understand commitments, and cheer me on has made a world of difference.

---

* Out of reverence for His name, I write G-d, rather than spelling it out in full.

I was the serious twin, and for me, life was quite significant. In some ways, my personal transformation mirrors the transformation of the acceptance of laughter as a worthwhile practice. My early years were spent in judgment, especially of myself, and I watched others play more than I participated. My husband Jan has been a role model of fun, play, and adventure. His love and support during this entire process have been invaluable.

Not only did our son Levi ask Sarah key questions, he laughed eagerly with strangers when I was still holding back. My daughter Leora inspires me with her easy and frequent smiles and giggles. My daughter Rina Chaya exemplifies the quote, "Imitation is the sincerest form of flattery." After bringing me as a guest laughter presenter to the high school gym classes she was teaching, she flattered me by becoming a Laughter Yoga leader herself.

Massive gratitude to Sarah for listening to me over the years and providing the safe space for me to learn to laugh freely again. I am delighted to be her creative partner and to join her in making a difference for so many.

And finally, thank you to the Creator of the Universe, for giving me so many opportunities to better myself, to be grateful, and for giving us all the freedom to choose to live fully, with joy and laughter, no matter what the circumstances.

About the Authors

Sarah Routman

Sarah's rich experience as a high school teacher and Executive Director of two nonprofits found its ultimate expression as a laughter professional. Certified as a Laughter Yoga leader and trainer, she has been named a Laughter Ambassador by Laughter Yoga's founder, Dr. Madan Kataria. Sarah is a sought-after keynote speaker and conference presenter. She wows audiences with her expertise, enthusiasm, and highly interactive laugh-it-out approach. After using laughter to help her overcome devastating personal challenges, Sarah felt compelled to share the message that laughter is a readily available tool for transformation and empowerment. For those Sarah trains, and those lucky enough to experience her deep, authentic, and highly contagious laughter, shift happens—in their personal lives as well as among their teams and organizations.

Also an accomplished artist with degrees in photography and English, her published photographs, poems, and paintings can be found in several books and numerous magazines. Sarah enjoys combining laughter with art to create enriched experiences of wellness and healing.

Rachael Siegelman

As a lawyer turned laughter coach, Rachael believes no matter how serious or studious you may start out, learning to laugh is a valuable life skill. Being a lawyer helped her to write this book, which contains hundreds of hours of her research. It has blossomed into a treasure trove of laughter lessons and includes a habit-based approach for anyone engaged in the study and practice of laughter.

Rachael is an accomplished student of personal development. She brings a deep reserve of knowledge from a vast number of disciplines into her laughter coaching. Rachael is inspired to empower all people to laugh for health and joy, especially teenagers, young adults, and seniors. Rachael continuously develops new *Laughter Games* with positive self-talk to enhance her students' self-care and relationships. She delights in helping people design and track their own laughter and play habits as they master the skill of laughing out loud.

Index

Underscored references indicate boxed text.

A

Abdominal breathing. *See* Belly breathing
Adams, Hunter Doherty ("Patch"), 214
The Alter Ego Effect (Herman), 176
Anatomy of a Laugh, 40
Anatomy of an Illness as Perceived by the Patient (Cousins), 74-75
Anxiety
　effect of laughter on, 74, 209, 214
　effect of Smile-Ups on, 46-47
Atomic Habits (Clear), 168
Autonomic nervous system, 50
A'wee Chi'deedloh, 185-86

B

Babies, 3, 49, 185-86, <u>235</u>
Baheti, RD, 218
Battie, William, 216
Belly breathing, 48-54
　benefits of, 50, <u>70</u>
　element of Laughter Yoga, <u>20</u>
　preparation for, 50-51, <u>52</u>
Belly laughs
　as prescription, 161
　benefits of, 67, 75, <u>82</u>
　physiology of, 49-50, 53, 69, 78-79

Belly Laughter in Relationships (Junkins), 182
Benefits of laughter. *See* Laughter benefits
Bereavement. *See* Grief and loss
Berk, Lee S., 76-77
Big Apple Circus, 215
Breathing. *See* Belly breathing
Brown, Stuart (*Play: How It Shapes the Brain*), 55-56
Burnout, <u>139</u>

C

Cancer, 43, 64-65, 147, <u>239</u>, 240
Caregiver laughter, 147, <u>221</u>
Celebrations
　adding laughter to daily wins, 199-200
　adding laughter to traditional holidays, 196-97
　annual laughter holidays, 189-196
　Awee Chi'deedloh, Navajo baby's first laugh, 185-86
　Fun Holidays Calendar, <u>198</u>
　Waraiko Ceremony, 186, 250
Children, resources for, 235-37
Clapping-chanting games, 91-95
Clear, James (*Atomic Habits*), 168
Clowns. *See* Medical clowns
Comedy, 121. *See also* Humor

Coping strategy, 6, 21, 143, 164, 222 (Service Industry)
Cortisol, 41, 71, 73, 121, 251
Cousins, Norman *(Anatomy of an Illness)*, 74-76
COVID-19 pandemic, 150-53

D

d'Arouet, Francois-Marie (Voltaire), 216
Declaration of a Laughter Champion, 163-64, 165
Deep breathing. *See* Belly breathing
Deep Survival (Gonzales), 73-74
Diaphragmatic breathing. *See* Belly breathing
The Divine Code of Life (Murakami), 217
Don't Send a Man to the Grocery Store (Robertson), 121
Dopamine, 73, 139
DOSE (Dopamine, Oxytocin, Serotonin, Endorphins), 73
The Dream Doctors organization, 215
Duchenne smile, 41

E

EGBOK! (**E**verything's **G**onna **B**e **O**-**K**ay!), 152, 173-74, 222 (Service Industry)
Emotions
  laughter's impact on, 4, 240-41
  physical effects of, 69, 73-77, 79-80, 119

End-of-life laughter, 148. *See also* Hospice
Endorphins, 4, 40, 41, 73
Eustress, 69, 77

F

Fight-or-flight response, 4, 70, 209
The First Laugh Ceremony (A'wee Chi'deedloh), 186
Fools are Everywhere (Otto), 212
Forester, Mike, EGBOK! introduction, 152
40-Day Laughter Challenge, 166, 178
Fry, William F., 207
Fun Facts, 216-17
  Burnout, 139
  Duchenne Smile, 41
  Gelatophobics, 37
  Jokes Turn Into Play, 20
  Laughter By-Product, Nitric Oxide, Wins Awards, 81
  Nervous Laughter, 28
  Stimulating the Vagus Nerve with Laughter, 70
Future of Laughter (Our Vision of), 220, 221, 222, 223

G

Gelatology, 207
Gelotophobics, 37
Gendry, Sebastian, 91, 238, 246, 251-52
Gene expression, laughter effects on, 217
Gissell, Izzy, 193-94

Global Belly Laugh Day (GBLD), 191-93
Goodheart, Annette (*Laughter Therapy*), 143-44
Gonzales, Laurence (*Deep Survival*), 73-74
Gratitude, 155, 156, 157
The Greatest Salesman in the World (Mandino), 158
Grief and loss, 16-17, 236-37
Group laughter, 19, 61-62. See also Laughter Clubs

H

Habits. *See* Laughter habits
Helle, Elaine, 191
Herman, Todd (*The Alter Ego Effect*), 176
History of Laughter, 203-17, 244-46
    documentary, 242
    humor (clowns, jesters), 211-12, 214-15
    negative views of laughter, 203-06
    religious views, 206
    theories of laughter, 209-212
Holidays. *See* Celebrations
Hospice, 120, 148-50, 221 (Caregivers), 237
Humor
    and health, 68, 212-14, 243, 251
    based laughter, 3, 121
    negative views of, 203-06
    philosophy of, 242
    research, 236, 240-41, 243, 244, 248-50
Humor Works (Morreall), 205

I

Identity creation. *See* Rachael's story
Imagination
    as focus of Laughter Yoga, 17, 20
    examples of, 62, 109-10, 131-32, 137-38
    stimulation of, 6, 86-87, 112-113, 117, 166
Immune system
    laughter effects on, 77
    research about, 243, 248
    stress effects on, 69
Inner Child, 56, 57, 65, 89, 115, 191
Inner Critic, 175
    life control by, 26, 28, 30, 33
    meet yours, 36
    silencing/disarming of, 7, 125-26, 127, 128, 168-69
Inner Voice. *See* Inner Critic
Intentional laughter. *See also* Laughter; Playful laughter; Purposeful laughter
    benefits of, 4
    in end-of-life care, 148
    in everyday life, 129, 199
    in Rachael's story, 163-64, 165, 166
    vs. spontaneous laughter, 4

International Moment of Laughter Day (IMOLD), 193-94
Intimacy, laughter's role in, 182-85

J

Judgment, suspension of
  as a rule, 61, 79, 89, 135
  creates safe space, 208
  enabling curiosity/play, 112, 164
Jump Starts
  Deep Belly Breathing, 51
  for resistance, 34, 37
  De-Stress with Grins and Giggles, 21
  Jiggling Belly Laughs, 79
  Time Yourself, 63
  to generate laughter 9, 117
Junkins, Enda (*Belly Laughter in Relationships*), 182-85

K

Kataria, Madan. *See also* Laughter Clubs; Laughter Yoga
  first mega-laughter party, 189
  founder, Laughter Yoga, 20
  laughing alone, 86
  no-judgment rule, 61
Keep Smiling cards, 44
King Henry II, 211

L

Laughercise, 77
Laughology (documentary), 217, 242

Laughter. *See also* Anatomy of a laugh; Intentional laughter; Playful laughter; Purposeful laughter; Shared laughter
  and genetics, 217
  as form of protection, 132-33. *See also* Laughter Shield
  as social skill, 182
  chemical effects of. *See* Dopamine; Endorphins; Oxytocin; Serotonin
  contagiousness of, 181
  healing with, 144-45, 214-16
  history of 203-17. *See also* History of laughter
  in babies. *See* Babies
  Our Vision of the Future of, 220, 221, 222, 223
  overcoming resistance to, 34, 35, 36, 41, 165
  survival and, 73-74
  universal language, 3
Laughter and Health (Walsh), 68-69
Laughter benefits, 219, 238, 239, 240-41
  chemical/physiological, 70, 73-74, 76-77, 81
  health and wellness, 67-69, 71, 77, 79-80, 213-14
  in business, 108, 157-58
  social, 181
Laughter Breaks
  Crumple Your Stress, 72
  Laugh Out Loud, 32
  Make Your Own Nitric Oxide, 82
  Pick Your Path, 175

Laughter Breaths, 50, <u>52</u>, 53, 56, <u>222</u>
   as part of laughter habit or plan, <u>165</u>, 170
   in speech and occupational therapy, 53
Laughter Buddy, 177-79
Laughter Cards, <u>223</u>
Laughter Champion. *See* Declaration of a Laughter Champion
Laughter Clubs, <u>20</u>, 177, 216
Laughter Games
   alphabetical listing of, 230-231
   categorized quick reference guide of, <u>232-234</u>
   creating your own, 105-17
   defined, 85-86
   goals and rules of, 61
   new games, <u>253</u>
Laughter habits
   cue 172-74, 199-200
   Og Mandino and, 158
   plan, 169-70
   stack, 170-72
   with a Buddy, 177-79
Laughter Online University, 91, <u>238</u>, 251-52
Laughter Participation Scale, 7-<u>8</u>, 31, 33, 35, <u>88</u>, <u>89</u>
Laughter poses
   akimbo (Superman), 53-54
   body-building, <u>159</u>
   pivot, <u>154</u>
Laughter Shield, 132, <u>133</u>, <u>134</u>, 135-39, <u>141</u>

Laughter sounds, <u>83</u>
Laughter theories, 207-10
Laughter therapy
   and cancer, <u>239</u>
   Annette Goodheart, 143-44
   and mental health, 246
   for relationships, 182-83
   for seniors, 250
Laughter Therapy (Goodheart), 143-44
Laughter triggers. *See* Triggers for laughter
Laughter Yoga
   creates safe space, 208
   overview of, 17-19, <u>20</u>, 56, 102
   research and resources for, 239-41, 245-46, 251
Lungs, 49, 69, <u>70</u>, 213

M

Mandino, Og (*The Greatest Salesman in the World*), 158, 168, 173
Mead, Richard, 214
Medical clowns, 214-15, 244
Miller, Michael (*Heal your Heart*), 79-80, <u>81</u>, 161
Mindset shift. *See* Reframing
Molecule of the Year, <u>81</u>
Mondeville, Henri de, 213
Morreall, John
   (*Humor Works*), 205
   (*Philosophy of Humor*), 209
Movement, benefits of, 108

Murakami, Kazuo (*The Divine Code of Life*), 217

N

National Institute of Play, 55, <u>247</u>

Navajo laughter celebration. *See* A'wee Chi'deedloh

Negativity, 126, <u>128</u>, 129, 164, <u>165</u>, 174

Nervous laughter, 27, <u>28</u>, 29

Nervous system, <u>70</u>, 77, 209

Nitric oxide, <u>81</u>, <u>82</u>

No-judgment rule. *See* Judgment, suspension of

O

Occupational therapists, 53

Otto, Beatrice K. (*Fools are Everywhere*), 212

Oxytocin, 73, 139

P

Parasympathetic nervous system, <u>70</u>

Permission slips for play, 190
  Have Fun & Seize the Moment, <u>191</u>
  It's Your Time to Play, <u>57</u>

Perspective shift. *See* Reframing

The Philosophy of Laughter and Smiling, (Vasey), 205

Philosophy of Humor (Morreall), 209

Play. *See also* Inner Child; Laughter Games, creating your own
  added to celebrations and holidays, 197
  as element of intentional laughter, 40, 54-65
  as theory of laughter, 210
  benefits of, 55
  free book about, <u>247</u>
  future vision of, <u>220</u>, <u>222</u>
  in relationships, 167, 183, <u>184</u>

Play: How It Shapes the Brain (Brown), 55-56

Play deprivation, 55, <u>58</u>

Playful laughter. *See also* Intentional laughter; Laughter; Purposeful laughter
  as a survival tool, 73-74

Post-traumatic stress disorder (PTSD) and medical clowns, 215

Professional laughers, 217

Psychoneuroimmunology, 76

Purposeful laughter. *See also* Laughter; Intentional laughter; Playful laughter
  formula for, 40
  to address stress, 131-32
  vs. humor-based laughter, 3-4

R

Rachael's story
  being a twin, 23-27
  breast biopsy, 46-47

Disneyland, 25-26, 39
Grandma Dina's death, 27-28
identity creation, 163-64, 226
influence of Annette Goodheart, 143-44
Laughter Champion, 163-66
Raviv, Amnon (medical clown), 215
Reframing
    as survival tool, 74
    games for, 233
    tools for, 6
    with cued habits, 172-74
    with gratitude, 157
    with music, 126
    with play, 55, 166-67
Relationships, laughter in, 88, 167, 181-83, 184, 185
Resistance (to laughter), 33, 34, 35, 36, 164, 165. *See also* Laughter, overcoming resistance to
Robertson, Jeanne *Don't Send a Man to the Grocery Store*, 121

S

Sarah's story
    childhood health challenges, 11
    divorce, 155, 132-41
    discovering Laughter Yoga, 17-19
    Grandpa Barney, 11
    Jacqueline, 13-17
Scott, Sophie, 182, 185

Self-generated laughter, 3-4. *See also* Intentional laughter; Laughter; Playful laughter; Purposeful laughter
Self-judgment, 27-29, 86, 263. *See also* Judgment, suspension of
Serotonin, 73, 139
Selye, Hans (*The Stress of Life*), 75
Shared laughter. *See also* Laughter
    benefits of, 181
    in relationships, 3, 19-20, 150-52, 181-83
    with Keep Smiling cards, 44
    with Laughter Cards, 223
Shore, Barry, 44, 244
Shriqui, Yaacov (The Dream Doctors), 215
Sickness and laughter. *See* Laughter, healing with
Skipping, 64, 65
Smile - Breathe - Play, 40, 56
Smile Buddy, 43
Smile-Ups
    as gateway to laughter, 41, 42, 43
    in daily life, 45-47, 145, 147
    to build laughter habits, 169-74
    with Laughter Shield, 136, 141
Smiling
    cards (Keep Smiling), 44
    chemical effects of, 40, 41, 73
    your access to laughter, 40-48
Social workers, laughter use by, 221

Solo laughter, 101-02, <u>175</u>
Speech therapists, 53
Speed Bumps, 9, 34-35
    Are You a Laughing Monk?, <u>188</u>
    Are You Play Deprived?, <u>58</u>
    Have You Met Your Inner Critic?, <u>36</u>
    Perhaps You're Thinking... <u>88</u>
    Remembering Joyful Moments, <u>78</u>
Spontaneous laughter
    effects on cortisol, 71, 248
    examples of, 11, 18
Stress
    books and research about, 71, 77, 236, 248, 251
    chronic stress, 9, 69-70, 73
    eustress, 69, 77
    free book about, <u>244</u>
    in cancer patients, 2<u>3</u>9, 240
    laughter habits and, 172-73
    Laughter Shield and, 132, <u>133</u>, <u>134</u>, 135-39, <u>141</u>
    management of, 131-32, 216, <u>233</u>
    nervous laughter and, <u>28</u>, 162
    physiological effects of, 73-75, 79
    smiling and, 44, 46-47
    work-related, <u>139</u>, 158
Stress hormone. *See* cortisol
Stress incontinence, 25
The Stress of Life (Seyle), 75

Stretching with laughter 53-54. *See also* Laughter poses
Sydenham, Thomas (Father of English Medicine), 214

T

Tension-easer pee, 25, 143-44
Theories of laughter, 207-10
Three Laughing Monks fable, 187-88
Triggers for laughter. *See also* Laughter Games, creating your own
    anxiety and stress as, 209
    humor as, 121, 162. *See also* Humor
    joyful play as, <u>54</u>, 56, 62, 65
    laughter habits as, 170-73

V

Vagus nerve, <u>70</u>
Vasey, George (*The Philosophy of Laughter and Smiling*), 205-06
Vision of the Future of Laughter, <u>220</u>, <u>221</u>, <u>222</u>, <u>223</u>
Voltaire (Francois-Marie d'Arouet), 216

W

Walsh, James Joseph (*Laughter and Health*), 68-69
Waraiko Ceremony, 186, 250
World Laughter Day, 189-90, <u>191</u>